84-559

BREAKING
OUT
OF
LONELINESS

Books by Jerry A. Greenwald
Be the Person You Were Meant to Be
Creative Intimacy: How to Break the Patterns
that Poison Your Relationships
Is This What I Really Want to Do?

BREAKING
OUT
OF
LONELINESS

~~~~~~~~~~~~

Jerry A. Greenwald, Ph.D.

Rawson, Wade Publishers, Inc.
New York

Library of Congress Cataloging in Publication Data
Greenwald, Jerry A
  Breaking out of loneliness.

  1. Loneliness. I. Title.
BF575.L7G73   1980   158'.2   79-67635
ISBN 0-89256-120-3

Published simultaneously in Canada by
McClelland and Stewart, Ltd.
Manufactured in the United States of America
Composition by American–Stratford Graphic Services
Brattleboro, Vermont
Printed and bound by Fairfield Graphics,
Fairfield, Pennsylvania
First Edition

To Brugh Joy
and
Carolyn Conger

Preface

Everything we need to know to resolve our loneliness and break out of it already exists within each of us. Those who feel plagued with the emotional pain of chronic loneliness may find this statement difficult to believe, for it implies that none of us needs to be lonely. Each of us actually creates and sustains our loneliness. When we see how we do this we can break out of our self-induced loneliness and discover new attitudes and behavior patterns that foster more nourishing, more meaningful living.

These more nourishing pathways from loneliness require no tedious struggle for insight, nor other laborious preparation. There are no preliminary steps to breaking out of loneliness. Rather, the issue is one of fuller awareness and self-confrontation. Any of us can begin or accelerate this process at any time in our lives. It is never too late.

Unfortunately, when we feel deeply lonely, we are usually convinced that our loneliness is either unalterable or can only be resolved through a difficult process, or that there is something lacking in us. Even more poisonous is the attitude that this "lack" must be in the outside world, so that we can only wait and hope. Especially when our loneliness seems chronic we may be sincerely convinced that our problem is insoluble, although we would love to believe otherwise.

Loneliness, then, is an active process in which we create,

activate, and perpetuate attitudes and behavior that, despite our good intentions, only lead to further loneliness. However, each of us can believe this only through the *self-validating* processes of our own experience. We cannot be convinced of this truth by someone else.

We live in a society in which loneliness flourishes. Most of us move about in our daily lives surrounded by people, yet we experience little feeling of personal contact. We complain of feeling alienation or indifference in our interaction with others, or of superficiality and transience in our relationships despite our best efforts. Most chronically lonely people agree with such comments about a lack of meaningful personal contact with others.

Since, when we feel lonely we are largely unaware of the specific patterns with which we create our loneliness, we feel lost in the black cloud that at times seems to contaminate every area of our lives. Our preoccupation with loneliness may become incessant, i.e., chronic. Then, even when we are not feeling the pain of actually being lonely, we are preoccupied with our fears and anxieties about possible future loneliness. We fail to enjoy and appreciate the nourishment and gratifications we do experience and instead tend to consider these as momentary distractions which merely postpone the loneliness we continuously anticipate.

While there are many characteristics that lonely people have in common, there remains a quality or style that is a reflection of the uniqueness of every individual. Similarly, the resolution of loneliness, the breaking out and moving on from loneliness, also differs from person to person. No "answer" is equally applicable or valid for all lonely people. As with other aspects of living, each of us who feels the pain of loneliness must discover the particular attitudes and patterns of living which we find most effective and meaningful in resolving our individual loneliness. Our ability to discover antidotes to our loneliness then becomes an integral part of the process of our personal growth. These antidotes to loneliness, the resolution and breaking out of loneliness and discovering how to move on toward a more meaningful and gratifying life, follow from a greater

awareness of the dynamics of chronic loneliness. Such awareness can enormously expand the possibilities of discovering
new directions away from loneliness.

Our ability to discover within ourselves and assimilate new
ways to nourish ourselves and others is limitless and can lead
us to our own inner wisdom. Growth itself, the active process
of discovering and utilizing our creative abilities, is full of joy
and love as we seek the most suitable way of breaking out of
our loneliness. These pathways are part of our inner reality
which, undiscovered, remains useless. Just as a person may die
of thirst in a desert while standing a few feet above an under-
ground stream, we cannot nourish ourselves as long as we are
unaware of our ability to do so.

Each of us is the center of our own existence throughout
our lives and we are responsible for everything we do. In reality,
knowingly or not, we answer to ourselves for our actions or lack
of action. There are always options available to us any time we
are willing to take responsibility. The philosophy of Gestalt
therapy, which is the philosophical underpinning of this book,
includes the broadest imaginable dimensions of human existence
and offers a natural, nonmanipulative approach to resolving
loneliness by moving toward an ever-increasing awareness of the
self and the infinite potential in each of us.

Contents

BREAKING
OUT
OF
LONELINESS

1

Introduction

SUE:

Ever since I can remember I've been lonely. When I was a kid I felt no one liked me or wanted to be my friend. I told myself that when I grew up it would be easier and there would be an end to my terrible loneliness. But as I grew older my loneliness continued and even worsened. At times I felt such desperation that I contemplated suicide.

Now I'm thirty-seven and divorced. My children are sixteen and eighteen and pretty much live their own lives. I have friends, interests, and am active in the community. Yet somehow, especially at night or early in the morning, I feel the same old pangs of loneliness that I have known all of my life.

Sunday I was alone all day, and I felt very, very lonely. It was the first time I felt real panic about getting older. Like what's going on in my life? What am I doing for myself? Mostly right now I feel scared. I've been in therapy a year. I'm getting tired of blaming my parents for everything. Yet, when I feel lonely and unloved I call them up and argue with them or accuse them of ruining my life by trying to make me into something I'm not. I just don't know what to do about my loneliness, so I lash out at them. I always wanted a big, close family. Somehow this never happened. I'd like to have people around, people who

care about me and approve of me. Now I'm really getting
sad. I feel like I've been lonely all my life. When will it
all end?

Each chronically lonely person could describe his or her own
version of a struggle with loneliness. Each would have his
or her unique pattern of events, experiences, and critical periods
of loneliness. Most could easily understand each other's dilemma since they share the pain of persistent loneliness.

All of us experience feelings of loneliness at times. Loneliness, and the fear of it, is the most frequent and widespread
cause of emotional pain. However, for millions of people
loneliness is more or less a continuous preoccupation. Millions
of others are vaguely fearful that their lives, too, may one day
be dominated by loneliness.

While many find the pain of loneliness tolerable, for the
chronically lonely, those like Sue who find their loneliness and
the fear of it more or less continuous, it is extremely painful
and, at times, unbearable. Loneliness is a state of emotional
deprivation characterized by feelings of alienation and psychological isolation. Lonely people live cut off from themselves,
others, and their world. Loneliness is manifested by deep inner
feelings of being unacceptable, unwanted, and unlovable.

Within each chronically lonely person are attitudes and behavior patterns which perpetuate loneliness. As long as lonely
people remain unaware of these or are unresponsive to them,
their self-perpetuated loneliness is likely to continue. When
we feel deeply lonely, we may believe we are simply victims of
circumstances, of the failures or inadequacies of others, or
countless other explanations. These are nothing more than
excuses which only enhance our feelings of helplessness and
futility.

Chronically lonely people are usually unaware that their
manner of relating to themselves and others is characteristically
toxic. The primary manifestation of their self-poisoning patterns *is* their loneliness. Most will deny this and may even
become angered or feel misunderstood since they have invariably devoted enormous effort to trying to cope with their

loneliness. In each instance, these well-intended efforts serve largely to alleviate the pain of their loneliness and avoid the inner confrontations needed to resolve it. Instead, they temporarily avoid or anesthetize the pain of their loneliness. Such patterns can become permanent.

Often we sustain our loneliness by attitudes and behavior patterns which are intended to deny or conceal it from ourselves or others but which only intensify our helplessness and thwart our latent ability to gain awareness of how we generate our loneliness. And, of course, these attitudes prevent us from discovering effective resolutions.

Chronically lonely people commonly deny their loneliness, appearing to be anything but lonely. When we have struggled with loneliness we have invariably developed elaborate defenses with which we manage to keep one step ahead of our fear of being engulfed in loneliness. This is done through enormous effort and activity and, in the long run, only drains our energies and avoids the necessary confrontation. Our life-style may be filled with patterns of manipulation of ourselves and others in order to avoid the confrontation with our own loneliness and our fear of being "found out" by others. We may even live out our lives and die without ever discovering that the potential for finding a creative, effective resolution to our loneliness existed within us all the time.

When we seek resolutions to our conflicts, the aspect of our behavior most obvious to others is often the very thing to which we are most blinded. Chronically lonely people see the resolution of their loneliness as primarily outside of themselves. ("If only I could find the right person to love me, my loneliness would be over.") The outer world, especially other people, is often their only source of gratification. They remain blind to the fact that the way to satisfy their basic needs is to be found within themselves. Each of us *is* the focal point of our personal existence and the primary source of our ability to gratify our needs. This same inner-oriented approach is also the optimal attitude for discovering how to obtain greater emotional nourishment from others.

It is ironic that when we are lonely we are usually most re-

luctant to turn inward and take a good look at our own attitudes
and behavior. Instead we cling to our externally oriented attitude: "What can I do to get others to respond to me in the
way I want?" We use our resources to create an endless variety
of manipulative patterns designed to evoke the desired responses. Convinced that *others* could give us what we need to
resolve our loneliness if they chose to do so, we then stay
trapped. Or we cling to our fantasy that the world would give
us what we want if we were different or could change. "People
would like me more and my loneliness would end if I were
older—younger--more attractive—wealthier—better educated—
more successful—more mature, etc."

As long as we remain caught up in these toxic manipulations
of ourselves and others, the real pathways to breaking out of
our loneliness remain unexplored.

Most typically we lack the self-trust needed to commit ourselves to the search for the creative resolutions to our loneliness
which always exist within us. We may even agree that while
this possibility is a most encouraging idea, it just isn't true in
our case. We may then continue to subject ourselves to the
whims of others and to circumstances. In this way we foster a
deeper sense of helplessness and futility as the inevitable frustrations of externally oriented attitudes reinforce our fear that we
are indeed inadequate, unlovable, and unworthy.

A particularly toxic aspect of this externally oriented attitude
is its tendency to define loneliness as a lack of satisfying relationships. This is the most deadly manifestation of this external
orientation since we then believe that the resolution of our
loneliness rests entirely on "successful" relationships, an as-
sumption that easily becomes an obsession. We may be successful in initiating relationships and yet find that our loneliness
and fear remain. The inner intimacy is still missing.

When we feel chronically lonely, our focus may be exclusively
on relating to others. This tends to keep us enmeshed in our
loneliness. We delude ourselves into believing that our self-
improvement programs—becoming a more attractive package—
can substitute for becoming more intimate with ourselves. This

is particularly deceptive since we may at times have been involved in intimate relationships with others and felt our loneliness lift. However, it is the quality, our way of relating that is our undoing. (Why don't my intimate relationships ever last?) For example, we tend to place an overload on our relationships as a reaction to our chronic emotional deprivation and frustration. It is difficult to be relaxed, spontaneous, and harmonious with those around us when we feel emotionally starved. Others, whether fully aware of this or not, sense our strain and urgency. The natural development of a relationship is severely hampered when we feel too emotionally deprived or manifest a compulsiveness in the manner in which we relate. Our relationships remain superficial and never reach real intimacy, or, when they do become intimate, they are short-lived, gradually coming to an end, or being terminated by traumatic rejection.

It is ironic that when we are not desperately needy of others and are open to relating to others without expectations, we are far more apt to enjoy an abundance of human contact and enduring intimacies. In contrast, when we feel deeply lonely, we usually have little to give in the way of nourishment *without* expectations of some payoff in return. Usually, we are not aware of the "hooks" (conditions) in our giving. Since we are unaware of the manipulative nature of our giving, we usually deny and are often angered by any suggestions that we are not giving. We are blind to the fact that it is the quality of our attitudes and behavior patterns that produces our loneliness.

Chronic loneliness may lead to a gradual emotional death when we remain unaware of the real issues. Meanwhile, we live in isolation, either alone or clinging to ungratifying or even destructive relationships because of our fear that, were we to let go, even of relationships we know are highly toxic, we would only doom ourselves to more intense loneliness and feel more isolated and empty than ever.

FEAR AND AVOIDANCE LEAD TO
EMOTIONAL DEATH. THE QUEST FOR
GREATER AWARENESS OF OURSELVES

AND OUR WORLD IS A HEALTHY
APPROACH TO LIFE. AT ANY MOMENT
OF OUR EXISTENCE WE CAN BEGIN
THE PROCESS OF BREAKING OUT OF
LONELINESS.

2

❧❧❧❧❧❧

How to Know Who You Really Are

When our fear of becoming more inwardly intimate is too threatening, we may convince ourselves that we can avoid self-discovery by finding someone else who will love us, accept us, and provide us with the outside intimacy we lack within ourselves. We try to convince ourselves that we can avoid our fears about what we imagine exists deep within us.

When we are unwilling to explore our deeper thoughts, feelings, and impulses, they become even more powerful and devastating *because* they remain unknown. The tendency is to become more and more fearful of ourselves and of being "found out" by others. A vicious cycle ensues, in which we are increasingly convinced that we *must* hide those nightmares, which conviction makes us ever more fearful.

THE LACK OF INNER INTIMACY IS THE SOURCE OF CHRONIC LONELINESS.

Those of us who have experienced periods of chronic loneliness can verify the fear that a Pandora's Box of unacceptable thoughts or impulses, as well as old feelings of guilt and shame for past unacceptable behavior, generate continual self-doubt about our acceptability and lovableness. While such inner thoughts are invariably fantasy, when we feel isolated and lonely we can torture ourselves endlessly while these doubts continue to block our way toward a deeper self-intimacy. The further tragedy of this Pandora's Box attitude is that we tend to live our lives as if these imagined inner horrors were true.

The more one lacks a sense of inner intimacy and self-love, the more one tends to avoid real intimacy when it is extended by others. Each of us has been loved and accepted by others *as we are*, yet we may remain unable to enjoy the nourishment of these intimate relationships for fear that should we reveal our "secrets," others will no longer accept us.

Feelings of chronic loneliness mean there has been a failure to accept ourselves for what we are, making it more difficult to trust our relationships with others. That gnawing feeling prevents us from reassuring ourselves that, if whatever we imagine is hidden inside us were to emerge, we would still be loved. No amount of reassurance can convince us of that if we have no love for ourselves.

> SELF-LOVE IS THE BASIS OF ALL LOVE.
> WE CANNOT ACCEPT FROM OTHERS
> WHAT WE ARE NOT ABLE TO GIVE TO
> OURSELVES.

Being intimate with one's self, which is simply a manifestation of self-love, means respecting the integrity of the self and every aspect of it, including whatever we don't like or may wish to change. We must recognize and love ourselves unconditionally, accepting negative patterns without judgment.

Inevitably it is through that awareness that we may move forward. At times we must choose between nourishing the self or others. Intimate sharing is a manifestation of love between oneself and others. However, just as any virtue can become a vice, so incessant nourishing and relating to others can become self-destructive when we fail to allow sufficient time and energy for ourselves. Intimacy with one's self requires solitude; during private times even loving interaction with others could be emotionally draining.

Similarly, even in the most intimate relationships, it is important to be aware of feelings and experiences that we find nourishing and do not wish to share with anyone.

WHEN WE ARE DEEPLY INTIMATE
WITH OURSELVES WE FIND THAT THE
ESSENCE OF MANY INNER
EXPERIENCES COULD BE DESTROYED
BY SHARING.

The full appreciation of an experience is sometimes dissipated by the very act of trying to share it. At other times, verbal sharing is simply not effective in communicating the essence of the experience. When we are frustrated by our inability to communicate effectively, the essence of the experience is apt to be lost. This frustration feeds chronic loneliness and unvariably implies a lack of sufficient time and attention to being alone with one's self and to experiencing the unique and essential kind of nourishment that these quiet moments can provide.

As long as we lack a self-accepting attitude, we tend to invest our energy in finding "flaws" and other "inadequacies," which we can make as psychologically real and devastating as we choose. Our inability to feel lovable hinders the likelihood of reaching out and accepting love from others. This is entirely a self-induced pattern for creating loneliness. There are no objective criteria for defining a lovable person. The rejection of intimacy with the self results in chronic loneliness. The fantasies we create tend to focus on how we should be, and they may become insurmountable obstacles against letting go of our loneliness. It's as if we continually have to *prove* ourselves lovable.

WE CAN NEVER *PROVE* THAT WE ARE
LOVABLE, BUT WE CAN SLOWLY KILL
OURSELVES TRYING.

The change that occurs *naturally* when we are interested in developing our potential as part of our growth process does not need proof, even though our accomplishments may be outstanding.

"It's incredible how suddenly and drastically my world has changed. I still can't believe this is happening."
This was Fred's comment as he told his therapist that,

without any warning, his second wife informed him she was in love with someone else and wanted a divorce.

A month had passed since that critical moment. He had moved out with only his personal belongings. Later that same evening, as he sat alone in a one-room furnished apartment, he felt a wave of panic. He had never felt so lonely before.

Fred was nineteen when he left his childhood home to elope with Stella. It was an unhappy marriage almost from the beginning, yet he was only ready to divorce Stella five years later, after he had been having an affair with Rosemary, his present wife. When he left Stella, he immediately moved into Rosemary's apartment.

Fred had always been aware of his fear of being alone. Even during his high school years he always had someone to whom he could turn should his current romance end unexpectedly.

He had felt secure in his second marriage, even though he knew Rosemary was unhappy about their relationship. He felt that she was so devoted to their two children that she would not deprive them of their father's presence. Now, suddenly left to his own devices for the first time in his life, his fear of loneliness enveloped him like a black cloud and he seriously contemplated suicide.

Any of us can be plunged into loneliness and despair suddenly because of events or circumstances over which we have no control. The death of a spouse or a sudden divorce after decades of marriage may mean the end of a nourishing support system on which a stable, secure life-style had been created. Waves of deep loneliness often fill this emotional and psychological vacuum. Similarly, catastrophic diseases, accidents, or financial reverses may mean the end of a particular life-style, resulting in a fear of abandonment and loneliness. This is a natural reaction, and we are all capable of dealing with it, and moving on.

When subsequent distress and frustration occur, it may call for the creation of a new life based on a new and greater awareness of the self. When, through inner intimacy, we have developed our self-esteem, self-love, and self-trust, we are more in contact with our inner resources and more capable of responding effectively to such dilemmas.

Failure to develop these capabilities may hurl us into a state of loneliness and despair from which we may feel helpless to extricate ourselves. For long periods of time we may feel overwhelmed and perplexed about what to do. When we lack awareness of our own resources and are frightened by the emptiness of our lives, we may brood about our misfortunes, be angry, look for someone to blame, or in other ways continue to be obsessed with what has happened. These and other such patterns are manifestations of a lack of self-intimacy leading to destructive forms of clinging to the past and avoiding getting on with life. It is a time of trial in which the solution rests on our ability to turn to our inner self. Groping for new footholds may be the only thing we can do yet, to allow ourselves to fall into a state of despair and futility leads only to chronic loneliness. When we are reluctant to confront ourselves with the choice to move out of loneliness, it is usually a direct manifestation of having failed to develop our own inner intimacy. In time of need, our inner intimacy can bring us into contact with our own strength to resolve our dilemmas, finish our mourning, and move on. This process of finishing with our mourning, moving on, and responding to the unfolding reality of the present is a way of breaking out of our loneliness.

THE FEELING OF SELF-LOVE, SELF-TRUST, AND INTIMACY WITH EVERY ASPECT OF ONE'S SELF IS THE MOST ESSENTIAL QUALITY IN BREAKING OUT OF LONELINESS.

3

How a Nourishing Attitude Can Liberate You

When we are lonely, we experience the routine events of our lives in an entirely different way from when we are not suffering from feelings of emotional deprivation—that is, continual isolation or meaninglessness has not poisoned us with attitudes and behavior patterns that filter out our joy, love, and vitality. When we feel stuck in a state of deep loneliness, our attitudes and behavior patterns become predominantly toxic, i.e., self-poisoning.

Each of us has within ourselves both nourishing and acceptable attitudes and behavior patterns which are part of our total identity at any moment. These have evolved throughout our lives and will continue to evolve. Nourishing and toxic attitudes and behavior are opposite manifestations of the same process. Nourishing behavior moves us toward life, while toxic behavior leads toward death, both psychologically and, ultimately, physically.

Toxic attitudes and behavior patterns characteristically create *unnecessary* psychological pain, frustration, and emotional deprivation. When we are in the throes of our poisonous patterns, we feel bewildered, angry, helpless, and hopeless. We see others apparently behaving in the same way but receiving much more nourishment, gratification, and response from others. We are unaware or have successfully avoided confronting ourselves with the difference in our underlying attitudes;

how we relate to ourselves and, subsequently, how we relate to others. The attitudes with which we search for the "answer" can be one of the principal ways we keep ourselves stuck. We fail to see the destructive attitudes and behavior with which we are literally creating and perpetuating our chronic loneliness.

A nourishing orientation makes us more aware of the need to attend to our inner selves, from which our attitudes, behavior, and responsiveness are directed. We are more in touch with our needs and have a greater readiness to relate to the world with an open, loving attitude that is largely nonmanipulative, i.e., without expectations. We may have just as many needs, anxieties, and frustrations as when we were relating in a primarily destructive manner; however, we are relating in ways that are more satisfying not only to ourselves but to others as well.

Positive attitudes are expressed in a self-love and self-trust, gradually enabling us to respond more readily and more effectively to others since we feel we have something to give *and* we enjoy giving for itself. Our way of reaching out, whether for our own needs or in response to the needs of others, has a quality of love and excitement which radiates outward. We are more apt to be experienced by others as nourishing.

In contrast, when our toxic attitudes prevail, we become lacking in self-love and self-esteem, since we become increasingly fearful that others could not genuinely be interested in us. As these attitudes become more extensive, the tendency is to shut ourselves off. Excessive suspicion or guardedness then creates more psychological barriers against the approaches of others. We emit a kind of negativity or anxiety which is experienced by others (whether they are fully conscious of it or, not) in a way that causes them to feel drained, restless, and distant, emotions which stem from an understandable need to protect themselves in some way from these negative attitudes. In *every* instance, the sense of uneasiness or discomfort others feel when our attitudes are primarily toxic is a reflection of our lack of a loving attitude toward ourselves, which appears to others as some kind of negativity.

One consistent manifestation of a negative attitude is the use of other people to give us what we want. When we fear that we lack the ability to satisfy our own needs and thus feel unloved and unlovable, we see the manipulation of others as the only way we can get what we want from them. This cannot help but indicate a lack of respect for the integrity of others, which then further poisons our interactions with them and results in deeper loneliness.

> Ward grew up with five sisters. His father died when he was six and from then on he was referred to as "the man of the house." His mother and sisters made him the center of attention and, as he grew older, he learned to play them off against each other. By the time he graduated from high school he contemptuously insisted that all women were to be used for his own selfish needs.
>
> He found the adjustment to college impossible since he had been so indulged all his life and was always able to manipulate his mother or one of his sisters into doing what he wanted. The frustration of being on his own and being expected to work persistently for high grades was too much for him. He wanted to go to medical school, but his efforts fell far short of requirements. Each semester he either dropped courses or failed most of those he completed; after two years he quit school completely.
>
> For Ward, women had always been the solution to any problem. He began dating only women from well-to-do families. He had been going with Betsy about six months when he asked her to marry him. Betsy was overjoyed and accepted. Ward then began to do one of his "numbers": for a week he acted depressed and refused to talk about his "problem," reassuring her of his love, telling her that his depression had nothing to do with her, and insisting that he would work it out on his own.
>
> Finally he allowed her to coax him into revealing that he was worried about making enough money to support her adequately. Betsy assured him that their two salaries were sufficient, but he insisted that he wanted her to have

all the nice things she was used to. His plan worked perfectly. Betsy spoke to her father, who owned a chain of auto accessory and tire stores and who was delighted to take Ward into the business as assistant manager in one of the stores. Ward and Betsy were married.

During the first two years he received a promotion every six months. Each promotion was instigated by Ward's complaints to Betsy, which she quietly passed on to her father. Ward would silently chuckle at his own cleverness, sure he had it made for life!

The crisis began to develop when Betsy gave birth to twin boys and could no longer spend so much time indulging Ward. Ward felt the competition almost immediately. Betsy's father was overjoyed at becoming a grandfather and, without any manipulation from Ward, gave him a large raise and a bonus to use as a down payment on a home. His job made few demands on him and he spent his time as he pleased. In fact, his father-in-law encouraged him to play golf at his club two or three times a week. He loved Ward like a son and assured him that he would provide for any needs. Ward acted happy and grateful but actually felt increasingly trapped and restless. It became apparent to Betsy that Ward resented the twins, but her efforts to resolve the situation were unsuccessful. Though she continued to give him a good deal of attention, Ward was not used to sharing her, or any woman, with anyone.

He began drinking and coming home late from the office. Then he began seeing other women. He would complain to them that his wife neglected him and did not understand his needs, even implying that Betsy was preventing him from getting close to his sons and that she was unwilling to share them with him. As usual, he was met with sympathy and understanding, and life again became tolerable.

When Ward met Elaine, he thought he saw a permanent solution to his dilemma. Elaine was an heiress who lived alone in a luxurious home, owned three expensive cars, and seemed to have more money than she could spend. Elaine clearly told him that she did not want to have any children. It seemed to be a perfect match. Ward decided to leave Betsy and marry Elaine.

What neither of them knew at the time was that they were playing manipulative games with each other. Ward, of course, thought that all he needed was for Elaine to fall madly in love with him and marry him, and that the two of them would live on her inheritance. What Ward didn't know was that her house, her cars, even most of the money she used for travel were provided by the family-owned corporation. While she could live comfortably on her monthly allowance, her inheritance was in trust until she reached the age of forty-five. At the time, Elaine was only twenty-five.

For his part, Ward had led Elaine to believe that he was a wealthy man, independent of his wife's family business. Elaine's tastes were far more lavish than her monthly income would allow and Ward seemed to be her answer to this problem.

It was too late when Ward discovered the truth. He had already told Betsy in quite a cruel manner that he had never loved her and that he wanted a divorce. Betsy's father fired him on the spot. While he was waiting for his divorce to become final, Elaine's family quietly investigated his finances and found out that he was almost broke. When they revealed this to her, she sent him a short good-bye note filled with angry and cynical humor and left on a six-month trip around the world.

It is to be emphasized that the concepts of "nourishing" and "toxic" attitudes and behavior patterns are descriptions of how each of us relates toward our inner self as well as toward others.

When we discover the simplicity and beauty of being nourishing to ourself and others, it is highly unlikely that we will be plagued by *chronic* loneliness. The essence of being a nourishing person is the ability to love ourselves and, in turn, manifest this same loving attitude toward others. This is the most effective safeguard against loneliness.

When we are accepting toward ourselves (recognizing how we are, but not necessarily having to like everything we see) and toward others, there emerges from within us an openness and sense of belonging that is so overwhelmingly powerful that feelings of alienation or loneliness begin to fade into the background. At any moment in our lives we can move from one orientation toward a more nourishing, self-fulfilling attitude.

Developing a loving attitude may mean recognizing that many of our long-established attitudes are negative. "Poisonous words" are now recognized as signs of toxic attitudes and behavior patterns, words such as "critical," "should," "success," "failure," "achievement," etc., are seen in a new context, in which we now recognize how they reflect judgmental or manipulative attitudes when applied to our personal relationships.

Toxic attitudes and behavior include all the ways which we use to hinder our ability to be loving and accepting toward ourselves and others *as we are.*

> AS WE PROGRESS TOWARD MORE
> NOURISHING ATTITUDES WE GIVE UP
> OUR EXPECTATIONS THAT ANYONE OR
> ANYTHING *SHOULD* BE DIFFERENT
> FROM WHAT IT IS AT THAT MOMENT.

This does not imply that we see ourselves or the world through rose-colored glasses or deny the pain and suffering that exist everywhere. Rather, we accept these "imperfections," in the sense that we acknowledge without judgment what *is.* There is no commandment that we *should* or *must* do something to change anything; instead, we recognize the simple fact that what is exists at this moment and cannot be changed. With this kind of nourishing attitude of acceptance, we can respond to the present in a far more gratifying manner. Our actions, and reactions, including our quest for the kind of growth and change we want, have the quality of moving on, breaking out of what we have now realized is non-nourishing, toxic, or obsolete. This nonjudgmental growth is the natural evolutionary process of the acceptance of our inner self. This is the essence of personal freedom. What each of us experiences as nourishing or destructive is not judged but is simply viewed as a manifestation of the different ways we, as individuals, perceive ourselves and our world. The natural growth process enables each of us to appreciate reality as *we* see it.

It is self-defeating to refuse to accept what does exist in our own experience at any moment, whether we like it or not. For example, continuous protest, complaint, and anger about aspects of our lives about which we can do nothing represents a toxic attitude. One of the best ways to become chronically lonely is to expend enormous energy without resolving what it is we don't like about our life patterns and without finding ways of breaking out of it. At times we may be caught up in negative patterns and be totally unaware of them and of all that energy we expend in a completely futile manner. And then we wonder why we're lonely!

A nourishing attitude, in contrast, recognizes and accepts what is. Then we respond as best we can and move on. For example, we may awaken with a hangover or stomach upset from too much alcohol or partying the night before. A toxic response is to rebuke ourselves for our indulgence, a way of being trapped in the past, or to make well-intended resolutions that we will never do this again, i.e., getting stuck with a fantasy about our future behavior. We can add to our suffering by moaning and groaning, being irritable, and again wasting our energy ineffectively and avoiding the acceptance of what *is*: in this case, the discomfort of "the morning after."

With a nourishing attitude we accept the existence of our hangover without wasting more energy complaining about, or trying to deny, the consequences of our actions of the night before. Full acceptance of reality creates the optimal condition needed to break out of the pain of our distress and end it. We are simply concerned with what seems the most effective action at the moment. No resolution is better or worse than another. We may allow our distress to run its course, experience it as fully as possible, and in this way use it as a learning process; or we may choose to ignore it and anesthetize ourselves with medication. This is simply a matter of personal choice, but either way, we have effectively broken out of our discomfort.

The loving quality behind all nourishing attitudes allows us to give up struggling against what has already happened and instead to flow with what is occurring from moment to moment, which is by no means a passive or lackadaisical attitude, but quite the opposite. Being aware and flowing with reality brings change and growth. We are using our energies efficiently since we are in harmony with ourselves and more able to respond to the world around us as it is now. The internal struggle, which always exists to some degree in all of us, between various, often contradictory aspects of the self is then minimal. We do not waste our lives resisting change or engaging in endless struggles against ourselves or others.

When we feel chronically lonely, we can be sure that various destructive attitudes and behavior patterns are dominating our lives. It is usually the case that our overall orientation is predominantly self-poisoning. Understanding the various patterns with which we create our self-induced loneliness can help us break away from loneliness and move toward the ability to achieve more nourishing ways of living and loving.

4

How to Know If You're Lonely

If we live our lives with attitudes and behavior patterns that create a state of chronic loneliness, we find a consistent and characteristic set of ways with which we inhibit, deny, or otherwise avoid our authentic selves and our natural way of being and relating. Feelings of chronic loneliness are a reaction to the emotional deprivation we create and sustain by our own attitudes and behavior. Still, most of us sincerely believe that circumstances of past or present are the main reasons for our loneliness. With a minimum of awareness, any of us who has known periods of intense loneliness will be able to identify with several of the feelings and attitudes that are the hallmarks of chronic loneliness.

All of us manifest nourishing and toxic attitudes and behavior, each set unique to the individual, though all the characteristics are not necessarily manifested in everyone. The attitudes and behavior of each chronically lonely person are manifestations of the way he or she uses these general characteristics.

Since all of us are destructive to some degree, we all create within ourselves a variety of unnecessary emotional pains and frustrations. When we feel chronically lonely we must first become aware of our negative patterns which cause our emotional pain and subsequent loneliness.

WHEN WE EXPERIENCE SEVERE
LONELINESS, WE ARE PERPETUATING
OUR EMOTIONAL PAIN, WHETHER OR
NOT WE ARE AWARE OF IT.

Intense feelings of anxiety and despair that are symptomatic of loneliness do not occur by chance. These are major symptoms of chronic loneliness. They reflect an inability to find meaningful nourishment in our lives. In our own way we are avoiding the action necessary to break out of our loneliness and move on. Until this confrontation occurs, the old destructive patterns are apt to persist and, most likely, intensify.

Feelings of chronic loneliness are a demand for change. It is a message from our self to our self to wake up and pay attention! Something is radically wrong. One of the main obstacles in breaking out of loneliness is our refusal or inability to acknowledge that it is through our own toxic actions and attitudes that we foster and perpetuate our loneliness.

Dan was in his early thirties when he lost an arm in an auto accident, following which he went into a deep, prolonged depression. He felt consumed by the fear that he was doomed to a lonely, frustrating life. He began to withdraw, especially from women, refusing invitations from old friends and beginning to drink excessively. He rejected others in anticipation of their eventual rejection of him. Many people cared about Dan but gradually withdrew as their efforts to relate to him met with increasingly hostile responses. He went through three years of agonizing loneliness before he was able to confront himself with the fact that he has been purposely isolating himself from others and that it was his responsibility to live in as nourishing and meaningful a way as possible despite his handicap.

The turning point came when Dan received word that Earl, one of his closest friends since high school, was dying of cancer and wanted to see him. The shock of seeing Earl was even greater than he had anticipated. Earl, who had been a lineman on their high school football team, now weighed only ninety-five pounds. He greeted Dan with a big smile and thanked him for coming. As Dan was leaving, Earl told him: "One thing having cancer has done for me is to make me appreciate every moment I am alive."

After Dan left, he wept profusely and then decided that it was time for him to stop feeling sorry for himself.

Each lonely person may have his or her handicaps, although usually not as dramatic as Dan's, but dwelling on them poisons the self and only fosters a feeling of helplessness and hopelessness.

> SELF-PITY IS A CHARACTERISTIC
> EMOTION OF CHRONICALLY LONELY
> PEOPLE.

Chronic loneliness produces such intense and pervasive anxiety and fear that it can permeate every area of our life, even to the extent that when we are enjoying ourselves and are feeling excitement and emotional nourishment, the threat of future loneliness remains and dampens our joy. This future-oriented attitude poisons our ability to live in the present. When we are afraid of loneliness we lose the excitement of our nourishing experiences by reminding ourselves (and usually everyone else) that: "It doesn't matter how good things are, since nothing ever lasts and loneliness may be just around the corner." Significantly, we fail to take the same attitude when we are lonely: that given half a chance, our loneliness, too, will pass.

> WHEN WE LIVE IN FEAR OF
> LONELINESS WE TEND TO ADOPT A
> DEFEATIST POSITION: THE GOOD IS
> ONLY TEMPORARY, WHILE THE BAD
> LOOMS FOREVER.

The Fear of Solitude

While loneliness is a state characterized by feelings of emotional deprivation, solitude is a kind of aloneness that is experienced as joyful and satisfying while offering many new areas of self-nourishment. Often, when we feel lonely, the idea that solitude can be joyful is an alien notion. Fear of solitude is not innate. Young children can become totally engrossed in solitary play, often for hours at a time. Most of us are aware of the need for privacy (another form of solitude) that emerges strongly in adolescence. Similarly, we feel an occasional urge to "get away from it all." Yet, when we feel lonely, our reaction to the prospect of being alone is usually anxiety and often panic; while the fear of solitude is characteristic when feeling lonely, we may discover that, when circumstances force us to be alone, we are capable of discovering solitude as a nourishing experience.

Sylvia was a thirty-five-year-old housewife with three school-age children. Her suburban life-style was busy, filled with taking care of her home, husband, and children as well as numerous social commitments. Throughout her childhood she had been extremely lonely. She was an only child whose parents both worked long hours. She felt as if she didn't belong anywhere. Sylvia was only twelve when she decided that marriage and a family were the only solution to her loneliness.

She and Mark were married the summer she graduated from high school. While she loved Mark, her primary reason for marrying him was her conviction that he would be a good provider and a responsible father. Their three children were born three years apart, as Sylvia had planned. She was contented with her life and congratulated herself that she had finally escaped her loneliness. Yet she occasionally felt a vague lack of fulfillment and restlessness gnawing at her, which she managed to push away without too much difficulty. Then, one year, the children were scheduled to attend camp for the major part of the summer, creating a rare opportunity for Sylvia and Mark to enjoy some time together.

Three weeks before the children were to leave for camp, Mark's boss suddenly assigned him to a two-month project in a distant city. Mark was genuinely sorry that they would miss this time to be alone together; Sylvia was quite disappointed and was not prepared for the growing anxiety she felt about being left alone. As the time grew near, she became panicky, pleading with Mark not to go, to ask his boss to send someone else. Mark insisted that he could not pass up the opportunity and besides, there was no one else in the company qualified to handle the assignment. Sylvia became increasingly depressed and began complaining of chest pains, which her doctor assured her were "just nerves."

The children left for camp, and four days later Mark left on his two-month trip. Sylvia was in a frenzy. She called friends, made a series of dates, and contacted people she hadn't spoken to in years. To some extent her efforts to avoid her loneliness were effective, yet she spent an increasing amount of time alone. During the third week of her "ordeal," Sylvia awoke one morning with a feeling of excitement and enthusiasm which astonished her. For the first time since her family had left she enjoyed sitting quietly over a leisurely breakfast, reading the newspaper. She took a long walk, something she had never done alone in her life. That evening she began reading some of the books she had accumulated through the years and had never read. Her depression lifted dramatically as she discovered that being alone was not the catastrophic event it had been during her childhood. She now felt elated at being free of her daily chores and was amazed at how sharply her energy level rose.

Sylvia had discovered the nourishment of solitude.

During the remainder of the summer she enjoyed her friends in an easy, casual manner and began exploring interests that she had previously been too fearful to consider. To her surprise, it was one of the most fulfilling periods of her life! Her exploration opened new horizons and prospects for her future. She realized that until then she had carried her fears from childhood and had simply assumed that being alone would bring back the dreaded loneliness she had experienced then. Now she broke out of the obsolete attitudes she had held onto for so long and allowed solitude to become a new and vital dimension in her life. Though she was joyful when Mark and the children returned, she began setting aside periods of time to continue exploring her newly discovered inner world and the delight of being alone with herself.

Sylvia's case is not unusual. The fear of loneliness and the idea that being alone is a curse often reflect our past experiences rather than present reality; yet, unless we actually experience solitude, we are apt to continue to equate aloneness with loneliness, and the fear of solitude will remain.

> WHEN WE ARE CHRONICALLY LONELY
> WE WILL NOT GIVE SOLITUDE A
> CHANCE.

The ability to enjoy solitude is an indication of growing maturity and self-acceptance since it reflects self-nourishment and self-reliance. This shift in attitude, from loneliness to solitude, is part of the process of our growth and deepens as we discover more of our limitless inner resources.

Embarrassment and Shame

It is easy to allow ourselves to feel that loneliness is a shameful and embarrassing sign of failure. We are taught that we should either be able to find an answer to any emotional pain or at least to be able to tolerate it silently. Above all, we are taught to hide our loneliness. The destructive attitude still prevails that open expression of emotional pain is a "weakness." We believe that if others were aware of our loneliness they would disapprove. The feeling of shame generated by such fantasies can be so intense that a great deal of energy is wasted in a constant effort to obscure the situation. Hiding loneliness can become a major destructive pattern in our life-style.

Martin was a seriously lonely man who had always been dominated by intense feelings of shame about his loneliness. He was a very successful lawyer and had hoped that his success would make him feel acceptable and finally convince him that he did not need to conceal his loneliness. While people appreciated Martin, and he had many friends of both sexes, his relationships did little to alleviate his deep feelings of shame. His loneliness continued to be a carefully guarded secret. He was convinced that if people really knew how he felt they would be terribly disappointed, even angry, at what he considered to be merely a facade of success.

After a six-year marriage he divorced a woman who loved him deeply but whom he did not love. He had hoped that marriage to someone who obviously loved him would make him feel more adequate and help him overcome both his loneliness and his feeling of shame about it. But the marriage was doomed to failure from the beginning. He and his wife had very little in common; she lacked his education and sophistication and he felt she stigmatized him with the people from whom he most wanted approval. Rather than face the shame of an immediate divorce, he decided that children might compensate for the lack of a nourishing relationship with his wife. They had two children eighteen months apart. Unfortunately, this only added to his guilt and intensified the agony of his empty marriage.

When he could not tolerate his loneliness any longer, he told his wife he was divorcing her. His feelings of shame and his fear of being even lonelier were all that had kept him in the marriage. Now he found it unbearably difficult to face his friends with the failure of his marriage and the additional shame of "abandoning" his children.

During college, before his marriage, he had escaped his loneliness by study and association with people who were always available. These relationships had little nourishment since he had settled for friendships with people who liked him without trying to initiate relationships with people whose company he preferred. Now he resumed the same pattern, stopping most of his usual social activities and avoiding his friends even though they tried to be reassuring. His loneliness became almost unbearable as he continued to do everything possible to hide it. With all his old feelings of failure and inadequacy, a new admission of intense loneliness seemed impossible for him. When he had to attend social affairs for business reasons, he would secretly hire a professional model as his date for the evening, a tactic which impressed his friends but left him with an even deeper feeling of shame. His dating was limited to women who pursued him, none of whom were attractive to him. When interesting women did approach him, and this occurred frequently, he would promise to call them, knowing all along that he wouldn't. His feelings of inadequacy were so overwhelming that he felt incapable of responding to the kind of women who might provide him with the emotional nourishment and intimacy he longed for. He was convinced that his vulnerability would only lead to further rejection and deeper loneliness when they "found him out." Martin had developed the life-style of a busy attorney who enjoyed the company of attractive women, lived in luxury, and had all the trappings of success. Only he knew the superficiality of his facade and the deep loneliness and despair he felt.

His pain became unbearable and he contemplated suicide, which emerged for the first time as an acceptable resolution. When Martin realized that he was getting close to taking his own life, he finally decided to try psychotherapy, which had been suggested to him in the past by his physician and several of his friends. He had always laughed off the suggestion. The thought of facing his inner conflicts and exposing them to another person had always seemed too embarrassing to face.

Therapy provided the turning point for Martin, even though he began solely out of desperation rather than conviction that it would help. Despite his education and sophistication he had clung to the idea that only "sick people" went into therapy. He was startled when, in response to his inquiry about whether or not he was crazy, the psychologist first reassured him that he wasn't, after which they laughed together about his anxiety. The psychologist then suggested that perhaps some of his other fears and anxieties might prove to be similar fantasies once he was willing to confront them!

Therapy was not easy for Martin. The therapist wanted to work with his feelings of shame and embarrassment, while Martin wanted to avoid these areas as much as possible. Gradually he began to risk expressing himself and initiating actions that were usually embarrassing. His therapist's constant statement would ring in his ears: "Feel free to feel embarrassed or ashamed or whatever, but do what you need to do for yourself anyhow."

Martin learned to be more open and honest in telling others what he needed and what he did not like as well. Now he was willing to reveal to others that he was lonely and feared rejection. He discovered that the more open he was, the closer people seemed to feel toward him—just the opposite of what he had expected all his life. Martin is still aware of his feelings of shame and embarrassment, but they no longer have the power over him they had previously. Martin has discovered that the more he risks, the more these feelings fade in importance. He now feels acceptable and lovable and is no longer lonely.

Past Regrets and Future Catastrophic Expectations

When we are lonely we tend to live in time other than the present. Our awareness of ongoing experiences, their meaningfulness and nourishment, is lost either in ruminating about the past or in being preoccupied with fears and anxieties about the future. We create more emotional deprivation and loneliness by our failure to appreciate and respond to the available nourishment that exists, even if we are unaware of how to find it in the present. It is ironic that we are so obsessed with the pain of feeling isolation and alienation that we are unable to absorb the emotional nourishment from our inner selves, as well as the external world, that could alleviate our loneliness.

WHEN WE ARE LOST IN THE PAST OR FUTURE, WE SUSTAIN OUR LONELINESS BY FAILING TO EXPERIENCE THE HERE AND NOW.

Most of us, when we are lonely, recognize how much energy we waste fantasizing about possible future catastrophes and agonizing about past misfortunes, rejections, and other traumas. In spite of this recognition, we may continue this destructive behavior, making ourselves unavailable for emotional nourishment *now*. Each existing opportunity to reach out for nourishment or respond to it is avoided, ignored, or deprecated, if indeed we are even aware of it.

Ted was thrown into an acute depression when, after ten years of marriage, his wife told him she was in love with another man and wanted a divorce. For several years their marriage had been deteriorating, and Beth had gradually withdrawn, becoming increasingly less interested in their relationship. Because of their disintegrating marriage, she had rejected his suggestion that they have a child. Ted blamed her refusal on the fact that she was thirty-three and felt unfulfilled. While she repeatedly tried to communicate to him that their marriage was falling apart, Ted refused to take her warnings seriously and concluded that she would get over it. He would block out her angry responses and he attributed them to her "moodiness." Beth was furious when Ted told her she would realize when she came to her senses that they had everything necessary for a good marriage. After Beth left, Ted at times felt suicidal, at other times he felt so angry he wanted to kill her. She adamantly refused to see him or discuss any possibility of reconciliation, and she repeatedly told him she was in love with someone else and that they planned to be married. Ted became obsessed with this rejection. For a while his friends were sympathetic and willing to listen, but as the months went by, they found it increasingly boring to listen to his repetitious grievances.

Eventually he began going out with women, but as soon as rapport developed, he repeated endlessly the story of his marriage and his version of his wife's deception and he would whine about how undeserving he was of such treatment. Over and over he told each woman how much he had loved Beth and how he would have done anything to make the marriage work. Frequently the women tried to tell him that they were getting tired of hearing about his marriage and would prefer to talk about something else. Ted would apologize, acknowledge his tendency to talk about his wife, and shortly thereafter resume his complaints.

Ted's obsession with his broken marriage was a way of holding onto the past. His refusal to break out of a relationship that had ended was evident in his comparison of each woman to his wife. Though he had been quite critical of her throughout the marriage, after their divorce he began to think of her as the ideal woman and no other woman could ever be a replacement for his distorted image of his ex-wife. Clinging to the past, he was blinded to the individual merits of each woman he met. As time went by, his loneliness increased, except during short affairs. These consistently ended when the other woman tired of his obsession with his ex-wife.

When he had been drinking he became paranoid, wondered if she had ever been faithful to him, and even questioned why she married him in the first place. As long as he clung to the past, unwilling to accept his divorce, he could not keep an open mind and open heart to the possibility of new relationships, and he continued to feed his chronic loneliness.

There is as much emotional nourishment in dwelling on past experiences, even nourishing ones, as there is in thinking about a meal eaten a month ago. Pleasurable reminiscing cannot fulfill our need for continuous present emotional nourishment.

Preoccupation with past regrets, misgivings, and resentments largely reflects what we see as a failure, our own or others', to meet our needs and is only an excuse for loneliness. Whether the reasons are valid or not, they become a blind alley that offers no resolution of those feelings of loneliness that exist now. Parents, living or dead, as well as past lovers and spouses, are particularly popular as scapegoats.

> Ted was unaware of the logical outcome of his hanging on to a dead relationship. Because of his deep fear of rejection, he built a wall around himself to keep people from getting close to him. He literally rejected each new, potentially intimate relationship, especially with women, by dumping his past unhappiness on them until they couldn't tolerate it any longer and, despite their interest in him, finally gave up.

By using past experiences as excuses for our loneliness we continue to cling to the past, ruminating about it and playing "if only—" games. As with Ted, this behavior pattern leads to a bottomless pit.

WE REMAIN CHRONICALLY LONELY
WHEN WE REFUSE TO LET GO OF
OUR PAST GRIEVANCES AND REGRETS.

Still more self-poisoning, though less obvious, is that while we are rehashing and clinging to those negative experiences, we are expanding them into a *new* past which we can regret in the future. To dwell in the past (since all of us can find experiences in which we felt mistreated, neglected, or deprived) easily can become a way of avoiding our fears, anxieties, frustrations, and insecurities about living in the present.

The corollary to living in the past is to live in the future. Here a similarly poisonous pattern of wasted time and energy occurs. Preoccupation with the future becomes increasingly toxic when we feel chronically lonely, since we center our fears and anxieties on innumerable possible catastrophes. Obsession with the future only enhances feelings of helplessness and despair, since no guarantees are possible. Just as living in the past is totally self-destructive, living in the future only saps energy that could otherwise be directed toward more nourishing living *now*. Future-oriented living offers the same subtle pay-off as living in the past. It is easy to be preoccupied with the future, so that our time and energy do not have to be focused on our fears of living in the present.

> LIVING IN THE PAST OR THE FUTURE
> MAKES US INCAPABLE OF GIVING TO
> OURSELVES AND OTHERS IN THE
> PRESENT.

The idea that any of us can ever insure ourselves against the possibilities of personal catastrophe that either leads to or includes loneliness only results in an endless and futile struggle. For example, if we fantasize that by dominating others we can assure the satisfaction of our various needs, we fall victim to the illusion that power or control offers a guarantee against emotional deprivation.

Many of us believe that figuring out a sufficiently skillful plan for the future and working hard to make it succeed will alleviate our loneliness. Once this fantasy has been accepted, we can then commit our time and energy to reach this goal. It is not hard to be sincerely convinced that this will bring about personal salvation, yet somehow, even when the plans materialize, the desired contentment and happiness may still be missing. Such well-intended manipulations of the self are a false resolution to loneliness and easily become an emotional straitjacket, hindering our ability to gratify existing needs. And so the same old struggle continues. If what we accomplish is not enough to resolve our loneliness, the next downward step is to become convinced that more success, more achievement, more of the same old pattern is needed.

If material success is seen as the key to successful resolution of our loneliness, we may work unceasingly pursuing this goal, creating our own brand of future-oriented living, which can provide an escape from ourselves and our fear of loneliness and isolation as long as we remain convinced that sacrificing the present will be worth it once we reach our goal. The fantasy remains that we can escape loneliness through success and achievement. Meanwhile, of course, our time is running out.

Impatience: The Easy Way Out

The pain and frustration of loneliness tend to make us impatient and impulsive about finding a solution. We are apt to look for that all-encompassing answer. Perhaps it's defined in a special relationship or something specific we can latch on to. This characteristic easy-way-out attitude avoids taking responsibility for how these "quick cures" affect the quality of our lives. The quick and painless remedy to problems is strongly reinforced by our culture, which fills us with false expectations toward life in general and, more specifically, toward ourselves and how efficiently we should be able to resolve our problems. When we feel chronically lonely, this attitude of looking outward for fulfillment is the most difficult, destructive, and frustrating approach. We tend to arrive at some decision ("I'll get married!" or "I'll move to another city and make a fresh start"), rather than focusing on the attitudes and behavior patterns within ourselves that are ultimately responsible for our loneliness. A desire for a final solution ignores the fact that reality is always changing and calls for adaptive responses within ourselves.

All of us want cures for our problems. There is a popular attitude to the effect that, if we are really okay, we should be able to find quick and effective solutions to our problems, and if we fail to do this, something is wrong with us. This unreasonable expectation only encourages the intense impatience and irritation we already feel about resolving our loneliness. It also enhances the likelihood that we will succumb to feelings of despair and futility when our efforts fail to resolve our loneliness promptly.

When Carolyn was twenty-four she inherited a considerable amount of money from her aunt, which she was sure would provide the solution to her lifelong loneliness. Carolyn had been overweight since childhood. All her efforts to diet were unsuccessful; she would lose a few pounds and give up. She was also very self-conscious about the size and shape of her nose. For years she had fantasized that, if she could lose weight and have her nose fixed, she would be popular with men and her loneliness would end. She quit her job, had surgery on her nose, and stayed for three months at a very exclusive weight-reducing ranch.

Carolyn felt as if she had been reborn. Her figure was slim and shapely and she couldn't have been more pleased with her new nose. By any standard she was quite attractive and, as she had predicted, men were constantly asking her out. Unfortunately, Carolyn still lacked a deeper feeling of self-acceptance and self-love—the real source of her loneliness. She gave herself sexually to a number of men in the belief that this would lead to a deeper love relationship and eventually to marriage, which she believed would be the ultimate answer to her loneliness, but these relationships turned out to be almost entirely sexual and each ended soon. Frustrated that her plan wasn't working, she began overeating. Two years later she had gained back all the weight she had lost and she felt lonelier than ever.

It is important to remember that patterns of self-induced loneliness have been created, sustained, and developed over the period of a lifetime. We usually ignore this fact, especially when our patience is exhausted, and we rush to find a quick answer.

Learning new attitudes and behavior need not be lengthy or laborious. It can actually fill us with excitement. However, discovering how to break out of loneliness is a process that is not developed overnight. In order to adopt a more realistic approach, it is essential that we give up the endless and utterly futile search for quick answers, automatic techniques, or other gimmicks that at best produce short-lived results.

Impatience which demands quick success is deadly. Any effective resolution of loneliness involves experimentation: the quest is to discover new pathways and new dimensions of ourselves. This requires an ongoing commitment to this more gradual process and a breaking out from the "easy answer syndrome."

Chronic loneliness is a manifestation of the fact that our natural growth process has been repressed or detoured. At any time in our lives, the reorientation of our attitudes is a gradual procedure. The more impatient we are when we are lonely, the more difficult it is to tolerate this step-by-step process. Yet the deeper our loneliness, the more vital it is to become aware of positive forward movement, breaking out from the patterns that have produced our loneliness.

5

❧❧❧❧❧

How to Stop Playing
Loneliness Games
You Can't Win

When we face ourselves and the world with a nourishing attitude, we accept the blunt reality that rejection is inevitable and we do not use rejection as an excuse to discontinue our quest for fulfillment. When we experience rejection, we should attempt to accept and tolerate our pain but not allow ourselves to get stuck with it. Rejection simply means that another person is not willing or able to give us what we want. While it is natural to react with pain or frustration when rejected, our reaction is far more intense when we feel lonely as well. Being rejected is then apt to be perceived as a verification of our fear that we are unacceptable and unlovable, that we are failures.

When we have felt that for a long period of time, we may become so phobic about the possibility of rejection that avoiding or denying it becomes a major preoccupation that dictates our life-style. Much of our energy may be wasted in futile attempts to defend ourselves from rejection. Behind this phobic attitude is the fantasy that we may never recover from rejection.

> WHEN WE FEEL CHRONICALLY
> LONELY, WE SEE REJECTION AS AN
> UNBEARABLE EMOTIONAL EXPERIENCE.

One poisoning effect of this attitude is that it readily becomes a self-fulfilling prophecy. Our attitudes toward rejection are learned in childhood where parental rejection may elicit feelings of being unloved and even abandoned. Children are relatively helpless in coping with rejection, for it means that the basic security of their entire world has suddenly been threatened.

> WHEN WE FEEL SEVERELY LONELY WE ARE CONTINUING TO REACT AS IF WE WERE HELPLESS CHILDREN IN A WORLD OF ALL-POWERFUL ADULTS WHO HAVE REJECTED US. WE CONTINUE AS ADULTS TO IMAGINE THAT WE ARE STILL TOTALLY DEPENDENT ON THE WHIMS OF OTHERS AND THAT WE LACK THE RESOURCES TO BRING ABOUT OUR OWN CHANGE.

The fantasy often sounds like this: "After all, if my parents didn't love me, why should anyone else?"

Most of us are intellectually aware of endless possibilities for new relationships. At the same time, when we have been rejected by someone with whom we have been intimately involved, it is natural to feel that we will never recover from the trauma and that we will never feel the same deep love in any future relationship. The common reassurances that we'll get over it do not change the reality of our experience. We are reacting to rejection on the basis of long-standing attitudes from our childhood that continue to tell us in adulthood that each new rejection is one more proof that we are unlovable and unacceptable.

It is ironic that millions of lonely people, from all walks of life, are desperately seeking meaningful relationships. Yet, because of their fears of rejection, they are mutually frightened of intimacy. It would seem logical that we would somehow manage to come together, acknowledge our mutual loneliness, and attempt to resolve it by risking intimate contact, but this seldom occurs. Each of us has created his or her own fears and fantasies that continue to convince us that no one else is as lonely, fearful, and desperate as we are. In this way we continue to starve ourselves emotionally while we live and work in close proximity to others who are equally lonely but remain stagnant in the same way. Our ability to nourish each other remains trapped in our fears, anxieties, and catastrophic fantasies about what might happen if we risk sticking our necks out to do the best we can to get what we want.

Integrating new experiences now is essential if we are to convince ourselves (and, remember, no one else can) that catastrophic fantasies based on past rejections and trauma are just that—*fantasy*. Those of us who sustain our loneliness through fantasy have actually programmed ourselves for rejection, and we become convinced that it will always be too devastating to tolerate when it occurs again. This is a self-fulfilling prophecy which reinforces the likelihood that the devastating effect we fear will indeed recur. Some chronically lonely people have programmed themselves for years, anticipating that moment when losing the love of a particular intimate will destroy them. ("If he/she divorces me, my life is over.")

There is no denying the pain of rejection. Nourishing people are able to mourn their loss, grieve, and gradually begin to resume their lives. Eventually, it becomes possible to be emotionally available for new relationships. This same rejection elicits in the chronically lonely a much longer and more intense reaction. The tendency to hold onto the past is an indication that we really don't want to let go of the pain. Clinging to past rejections can be a way of protecting ourselves from again becoming vulnerable to the possibility of new rejections. The known, even if it is terribly painful, appears easier to tolerate than the unknown. And yet, ultimately, to hide from the vital need we all share, i.e., the need for fulfilling relationships, is far more painful in the long run.

The Emotional Cripple Fantasy

When we have suffered chronic loneliness for a good part of our lives, it usually means that we have failed to discover our inner potentials. We have also failed to discover that these potentials are more than ample for resolving our loneliness.

Instead, we continue to torment ourselves with an overwhelming feeling of helplessness, a self-poisoning attitude which reinforces an "other-oriented" attitude in which we give away our personal power to others: "Someone save me or I'll perish." We continue the patterns with which we cripple ourselves emotionally. We learn to become master manipulators and we use our energies to get others to give us what we need, rather than learning how to do it by using our own resources.

Many patterns learned in childhood foster this attitude toward loneliness. When parents are excessively helpful in solving their children's conflicts, or trying to "protect" them from the painful realities of growing up, they foster this dangerously crippling attitude that can last a lifetime.

The important characteristics of self-reliance, self-discipline, and concentration are often stifled by excessively permissive, indulgent parental attitudes, which fail to allow the necessary psychic space children desperately need to grow and discover how to cope with their emotional pain on their own. Their natural ability to learn to tolerate frustration, disappointment, and rejection is thwarted. Little wonder, then, that in adulthood the tendency is to feel and act like emotional cripples.

Another dangerous parental attitude centers on so-called constructive criticism. It is easy to believe that those well-intended comments can only be helpful. This approach, if over-used, may usurp a child's need for an environment that is psychologically accepting. It is important to encourage in children the attitude that it is all right to grope and to err in the process of learning to be on their own.

> PERSEVERANCE IN THE FACE OF
> FRUSTRATION AND DISAPPOINTMENT IS
> ESSENTIAL IN LEARNING HOW TO
> COPE WITH LIFE.

It is these and other toxic attitudes that enhance our anxiety about being alone and set the stage for loneliness. If we were taught to lack self-trust, and if we continue to believe that we need to be validated by others, despite the resentment we feel, then playing the game of "emotional cripple" can be gratifying for long periods of time. We can always try to get others to do our work for us. Yet, behind it all is the dread of loneliness, that one day no one may be around to lean on.

Richard, an only child, was raised by two demanding, perfectionist parents who constantly criticized him for his imperfections. "Richard, why can't you do anything right?" was the prevailing theme. Over and over he would resolve to try harder to please his parents so that he could finally win their approval and with it (so this fantasy always goes) their love. Yet his best efforts repeatedly failed. Whatever he did well, and he had many talents, was dismissed as expected. Anything less was met with criticism, which his parents justified as being for his own good.

Throughout his childhood he had no idea of how excessive the nature of his parents' demands were. When he visited friends and saw a more accepting, less demanding atmosphere, he concluded that his friends' parents were rather slipshod and negligent. As he grew older, he began to feel increasingly frightened and insecure about the prospect of going out into the world on his own. He felt so inadequate, so unable to satisfy his parents' expectations that he wondered how he would be able to survive without them.

In his freshman year of college he met Estelle, whose attitudes were remarkably similar to his parents'. She too was a perfectionist and her critical nature seemed reasonable, even helpful, to Richard.

Finding real comfort in this, he continued in the same role with Estelle that he had learned with his parents. Just as he had learned to turn to his parents for advice, even about trivial matters, he now turned to Estelle and she seemed quite willing to assume his parents' role. To Richard this was an indication of her love for him.

Two years later, Richard and Estelle married and their home life was remarkably similar to what he had always known. He became very successful in the business world: in his early thirties, he was a high-salaried executive in a large corporation. There, for the first time in his life, he received praise and recognition. Gradually he began to resent his wife's criticism and advice. Sometimes he wished he hadn't married her. He seriously considered leaving her, but his old fear about being on his own remained overwhelming.

Richard lived as if he were an emotional cripple. His parents had so controlled his own sense of power and integrity while he was a child that he had yet to learn what it was like to live as a self-determining adult. It was almost inevitable that he would select a partner who would dominate him. Like his parents, he saw Estelle as someone who really knew better than he did what was best for him. His fear that without her his success would fade away continued. At the same time his resentment grew as he became more aware of the appreciation and recognition, both professional and social, that he received from others.

Circumstances intervened that changed his lifelong attitude of seeing himself as an emotional cripple. It began when Estelle was called home to take care of her ill mother who was expected to live perhaps a month, certainly no longer than a year. Richard's initial reaction was panic that his wife would be a thousand miles away. His resentment faded, and his fear and anxiety about being on his own were almost unbearable. Estelle was away for over five months, during which time Richard faced various crises and decisions. He tried in vain to find someone he could trust who would advise and counsel him, but for the first time in his life, no such person was available. Phone conversations were ineffective since Estelle was so totally concerned with taking care of her mother and so resentful when Richard persisted in bothering her about "trivia" and running up huge phone bills.

The turning point came when he received a very attractive offer from a rival firm. His anxiety about making a decision to give up a secure position for something new was so intense it bordered on panic. In the past he would have dumped the whole matter on his wife. He would have moaned and groaned and argued until she finally convinced him of what in her opinion was best for him. He was totally unsatisfied with her glib statement to "forget it," and she was unwilling to persuade and cajole him to the point where he was convinced she was right.

He made the decision to join the new firm and, predictably, felt enormous anxiety about all the uncertainties of a new situation. It was a painful ordeal for Richard to handle a major decision entirely on his own, but by the time Estelle returned, he had worked through most of his anxieties and felt stronger and more secure than ever. Most important, he realized that, having taken the necessary risk of making up his own mind, he felt the thrill of being in charge of his own life for the first time.

The Avoidance of Learning

When we are caught in the web of chronic loneliness we are usually unaware of how we interact with others. Therefore, our ability to learn from our experiences and to become more effective in developing nourishing relationships can be blocked. For example, loneliness can leave us feeling so desperate for intimate contact that we may lose our ability to discriminate between the positive, nourishing responsiveness of others and those responses which are phony, manipulative, and toxic. We then fail to recognize the difference between these nourishing and toxic attitudes in others or how to modify our own behavior in a more positive manner.

CHRONIC LONELINESS HAMPERS OUR
ABILITY TO LEARN.

Often we may be startled to hear how others perceive us. For example, chronically lonely people may be unaware that others resent their boisterous attitude or the plastic smile that never leaves their face. They may be totally unaware of their hostile humor, their criticism, or the other ways in which they turn people off.

There is always the possibility of learning more about ourselves and how others react to us, but as long as we avoid paying attention to ourselves and to others, new learning is stifled. For example, it is a fact that the lonely tend to avoid eye contact. They expect rejection to such an extent that they assume that the feared rejection and hostility actually exist. They continue to relate on the basis of old patterns learned in the past; actually it is they who are doing the rejecting. To the extent that we blindly cling to our habitual attitudes and behavior patterns, our ability to learn from new experiences is severely hampered.

The universe is not hostile; it is available, hospitable. But as long as we avoid using our senses, we continue to imagine that we are surrounded by the hostility and rejection we fear so much. Despite our frustrations, we are blocked from finding the gratifications we so desperately need.

Ignoring reality is a characteristic defense when we feel chronically lonely, a manifestation of a learning disability. This attitude of overlooking the many clues that could come into our awareness is typical of the failure to use our inner resources to discover those nourishing sources that are always available.

Experimenting with new and different attitudes and behavior which might lead to effective resolution of loneliness produces anxiety. We always encounter an element of fear and psychic pain when we seek to expand our awareness. Yet, expansion is vital in order to resolve our loneliness. Refusing to learn simply because something might be discovered that seems too threatening to face perpetuates a vicious cycle of ineffective behavior.

Rita was an unusually attractive woman who longed for marriage and children. Despite a great deal of dating, this possibility never seemed to develop. At times she sensed vaguely that there was something about her way of relating to men that aborted the likelihood of this kind of intimacy.

"It suddenly dawned on me one day that once I go to bed with a man, sex takes over. We go to fewer and fewer parties and restaurants and gradually we spend less and less time with other people None of them seemed interested in knowing *me!* I wondered if this was my imagination or whether there was really something to it. At the time I was dating several men; I decided to try an experiment. I would suggest that we cut out the preliminaries and go straight to bed. Then if we wanted to do something afterward, fine.

"I found that not only was this acceptable, but that in each instance the man I was dating preferred it. They wanted sex and were not looking for anything else."

What she had been ignoring for so long now became obvious. Often, men would tell her that they were not interested in any permanent relationship, that they simply wanted to be friends and enjoy a sexual relationship. Rita avoided confronting herself with the implications of such statements. Instead she clung to an old notion that this was the way all relationships start, that eventually the "right man" would change his mind and would also want an exclusive relationship. Rita simply didn't listen to what the men in her life were telling her.

Now she confronted herself with the fact that as long as she was going to date men who only wanted sex, the likelihood of finding the kind of relationship she wanted remained minimal. Now she also realized that the casual dating of many men took a great deal of her time, often leaving her unavailable to new men who wanted to socialize.

As she realized these old relationships were not satisfactory, she began to break out of them. She gave up her ritualistic behavior of going to bed with each man immediately in order to minimize her anxiety about pressure if she said no. She even decided that she would risk "losing" the right man who might not call again if she rejected his sexual advances. Rita was amazed to find what a difference this made in her dating: "It's as if I've discovered a new breed of men. They see me as a person and, to be quite honest about it, I also see them more as people. Actually, the men I am dating now are much more interesting and exciting."

Rigidity

Rigidity and ignorance are toxic patterns which reinforce each other. As with ignoring reality, rigidity helps us ward off the fears and anxieties that we imagine would overwhelm us if we opened ourselves to the possibilities that exist in present reality.

> RIGIDITY CAUSES US TO RELATE TO
> OURSELVES, OTHERS, AND THE WORLD
> IN GENERAL WITH PREJUDICES BASED
> ON PRECONCEIVED IDEAS WE
> LEARNED LONG AGO.

When we limit our perceptions to those which fit into our preconceived notions of reality, we actually reinforce attitudes and behavior patterns learned in the past, which may well be obsolete in the reality of the present. We may insist that opening ourselves to seek more nourishing experiences would only be asking for more of the same old pain. We may sincerely believe that we are only being prudent in maintaining our barriers against both greater contact with our inner selves and with others.

The nourishing self, which exists within each of us throughout our entire lifetime, relentlessly strives for expression. Regardless of how rigidly we maintain our inner protective boundaries and cling to the safety that comes with old familiar patterns, on the same level we continually experience a variety of feelings, needs, and desires which are not being satisfied. Yet when we feel lonely and fearful of something new and different, we tend to reject even positive experiences that don't fit our preconceived notions. For example, when someone reaches out with an open, loving attitude, we may look for some ulterior motive or decide that the other person doesn't know what we are really like or they wouldn't be so loving. In this way we manage to sustain our rigidity and preserve our self-induced loneliness.

Rigidity as a reflection of loneliness is often verified by our reaction when others suggest that we are rigid or dogmatic. Usually the response is intensely emotional and/or defensive, suggesting that these comments touch something frightening that has been deeply ingrained in us for years.

Well-meaning friends and relatives may persist in offering advice and suggestions when we have been feeling lonely for some time. Such attempts, however sincere, eventually sound like a debate between a protagonist and antagonist. It is characteristic when feeling lonely to go round and round in our minds trying to analyze our loneliness. Usually we have ruminated over every possible solution we can conceive of, many of which we may have tried. In any case, our responses to suggestions from others are, to say the least, almost invariably lacking in enthusiasm, because when we are lonely we are also frightened and have closed ourselves off as protection against the unknown. We give lip service to the "helpfulness" of others or we respond with silence or polite agreement. At other times we may use such occasions to be argumentative about the usefulness of the suggestions.

This easily becomes a toxic game in which our caring friends get sucked into a futile struggle to finally come up with something that will provoke a positive reaction of appreciation, hope, or excitement. ("Hey, I never thought of that!") Such efforts are almost invariably doomed to failure, because when we feel deeply lonely it is difficult to be open to anything new, even though we usually insist that we are! The real resolutions, those we have not tried, call for a new evaluation of attitudes and behavior that often appears too threatening. So, our fear and anxiety keep us stalemated in our loneliness. And as long as we continue to maintain security by rigidly clinging to the familiar, we are not going to let anyone talk us into giving it up.

I Don't Need Anyone But You

The notion that emotional maturity means becoming an island unto one's self, that then we don't need others, is simply not true. Similarly, many chronically lonely people insist that a single intimacy is enough to satisfy all their needs for human relationships. This difference in attitude between nourishing and toxic people's approaches to their need for relating is il-lustrated in the following examples:

TOXIC TOM:

"Since Mary and I broke up three months ago, I've been feeling a lot of loneliness and it really hurts. I keep calling her but she won't have anything to do with me. I want to try again, even though she keeps telling me she's had it. She insists that three years of living together with all the hassling we had is enough. Now she's met someone new she's thinking about living with. But I'm not going to give up. Maybe she'll change her mind. After all, one of the things that therapy has taught me is that I'm not such a bad guy. Meanwhile, I'm fixing up the house and getting things done that I've postponed for months. I'm working harder at my job and I'm making more money than ever. But my loneliness is getting worse. When I do date other women I let them know the relationship isn't going any-where—that I'm waiting for Mary to change her mind. When I sleep with another woman I feel resentful that she isn't Mary. I still think she'll change her mind and I'll be there when she does. I'm still involved with Mary, although we have broken up, and I really don't want or need to get involved with anyone else."

Tom is sincere in his way of dealing with his breakup with Mary. However, he is poisoning himself by ignoring what Mary has told him repeatedly and explicitly, though, of course, it's possible Mary will change her mind. However, the toxic aspect of Tom's approach to his loneliness is his insistence on waiting for her, which sabotages any chances for new relationships. In addition, he uses his other activities as busywork—both perfect ways of avoiding his loneliness and staying isolated from others.

In the following monologue, Nancy expresses a more nourish-ing attitude about her loneliness. Like Tom, she has just broken up with someone she has been living with. For some time Burt had been increasingly restless. Finally, he decided to quit his job, sell all his possessions, and travel alone for a year or two until he "found himself." He asked Nancy to wait for him. They had always had a good relationship, which he suggested they could resume when he returned. He even hinted that his fantasy of extended travel might not turn out to be as exciting as he hoped and he might return in a few months. Burt left Nancy with the pain of loneliness and a deep sense of loss.

NANCY:

"It's really hard being without Burt. Our relationship was the most intimate and most gratifying I've ever known. I could see there was something restless about him, I knew that at some point it was likely we would go our own ways. I'm not going to kid myself that I can forget Burt that easily. At the same time, I'm letting everybody know that Burt and I have broken up and that I'm dating. Dating is really hard. There are times when I don't date because it's just too painful. It's hard to keep Burt out of my mind when I'm with another man. Some of my solitary time I enjoy and I realize that I missed it while Burt and I were so involved. I date some of my ex-lovers, but I know these relationships are part of the past. I can't do anything about Burt's plans for the future. But I'm not going to wait and hope that he might come back soon or find that he misses me too much. I used to poison myself in the past with such hopes when a relationship ended. Burt's restlessness is a part of him and he likes it. It's a challenge to him. I, on the other hand, want a one-to-one relationship that I can build into a more enduring life-style, one that I could never realistically hope for with Burt. It is painful to know that I wanted it with him and won't have it. But I don't want to avoid facing up to what I feel I must do.

Nancy's statement was filled with pain and sadness mixed with healthy determination. She has come to appreciate her own strength and can allow herself to feel all her emotions, including frustration. She does not need to blind herself to the past reality of the relationship as she knew it. Instead, she has accepted her need to let go of Burt, whether or not he returns. She trusts herself enough to realize that this is the best way for her to open herself to a new relationship where she has the opportunity to find what she is looking for.

Manipulation Versus Authentic Relating

All of us manipulate other people, whether we are aware of it or not. We try to get them to do what we want in ways that are devious, misleading, or otherwise lacking in honesty. Loneliness often motivates us to become master manipulators. While manipulation may be successful for considerable periods of time, in the long run it only leads to greater loneliness. We may take nourishment from others while giving little in return, but ultimately others are apt to become weary of the lack of reciprocation.

Manipulation is absolutely the opposite of intimacy and erodes the nourishing aspects of any relationship. Typically, when we have lived largely in the throes of loneliness, manipulation becomes so much a part of our relations with others that sooner or later it becomes too overwhelming for any nourishment to counteract.

> MANIPULATION IS THE MOST
> DANGEROUS THREAT TO THE
> EMOTIONAL NOURISHMENT WE ALL
> NEED.

This is one of the hallmarks of the chronically lonely person. The tragedy is that we may live our lives convinced that manipulation is the only way to get any kind of sustenance from others.

Projections of our inner fears and harsh self-judgments onto others can poison every encounter where the possibility of intimacy might otherwise exist. Out of fear, manipulation is often chosen as safer than authenticity.

> OUR OWN JUDGMENTAL ATTITUDE
> TOWARD OUR THOUGHTS, FEELINGS,
> IMPULSES, AND PAST DEEDS IS
> PROJECTED ONTO OTHERS, SO THAT
> WE EXPECT TO BE JUDGED.

"You have no idea how lonely it is to always have to be 'one.' " This was the opening statement that a member of a popular rock band made during a weekend encounter group.

"I'm in great demand by people who don't have any idea who I really am. They want to know that guy they see performing on the stage. If some lady makes it with me, it's a personal triumph she can tell her friends about. Now I know why women get so angry when some guy cons them when he's really only interested in their bodies. A lot of guys envy me. They ask me: 'Isn't it great to go to bed with a different woman every night?' At first it was, but after two years, let me tell you that being on tour, constantly moving from one town to another, is lonely as hell."

The more manipulative we are, the more we tend to see others as largely sources of gratification, appreciated only for their usefulness. This attitude of "usefulness" dominates our way of relating to others. When we feel deeply lonely we may utilize the same attitude to alienate ourselves from a deeper intimacy toward our inner self as well, because our self-worth rests on our ability to be useful or valuable to others. We try to make ourselves into objects in order to become a more "attractive package." We may use enormous energy becoming a valuable commodity in strong demand.

Giving as a Manipulation

The confusion we may feel about our loneliness often stems from what we see as our considerable efforts to give to others. However, our "giving" may contain a subtle hook; an expectation that a positive response should be forthcoming in return. Relating with an expectation that others should respond to our giving in some positive fashion is a prime example of how we create a pattern of self-induced loneliness. Such expectations hamper our ability to become aware of how others actually do respond to us. A phony relationship of mutual manipulation is usually the consequence when two people relate to each other primarily on the basis of each other's expectations.

In manipulative "giving" a person may relate by doing things for others, being available when others need help, giving gifts, extending invitations and so forth, and then feeling disappointed, disillusioned, or resentful when the other person does not respond according to his/her expectations. In this way the lonely person creates a one-sided contract, which, it is assumed, the other person will honor.

CONTRACTS DISRUPT THE ESSENCE OF
REAL GIVING.

Even though entirely fantasized, expectations imply that a contract exists. The more expectations we have, the more likely it is that our relationships will be based on manipulative games that are apt to become increasingly destructive rather than leading to real intimacy.

AUTHENTIC GIVING IS UNCONDITIONAL.

It is "casting the bread upon the water." We give because we feel a need to give. Authentic giving is an end in itself without expectation about what, if any, response will follow.

UNCONDITIONAL GIVING IS RARE
WHEN WE ARE IN A STATE OF
CHRONIC LONELINESS.

While giving unconditionally is the ultimate in authentic, intimate relating, and in that sense is a selfless act, it does not at all imply that we become selfless, that we don't have our own needs. This altruism is possible for some saintly people, but surely not for most of us. Acting as if we don't need anything is usually a well-intended effort that quickly becomes a fruitless game of giving out of guilt, giving to atone, or some form of self-sacrifice. But there is no connection between such well-intended efforts and unconditional giving. They are not ways of giving simply for the joy of giving.

"I love giving to others and making them happy. It gives me great joy to please someone." This was Ralph's comment about himself during an intimate conversation with some close friends. Ralph saw himself as a "giver" and his friends agreed with him. He was only vaguely aware of his subtle anticipation that he would be appreciated and in turn given to as a consequence of his own generosity.

When one of his friends commented that he seemed to expect an appropriate response to his giving, Ralph became angry, feeling he had been unfairly accused of something. That night he was restless and unable to sleep. He began to ponder the discussion of the evening. It had been almost a year since his divorce and he was still recovering from the emotional wounds of that relationship. He had been deeply in love with Doris and enjoyed giving to her in various ways. Now he recalled the frequent depressions he had felt during their marriage. While Doris had been genuinely appreciative of the way Ralph gave to her, he suddenly realized that there was something he wanted from Doris which was never forthcoming—her giving to him. Now Ralph realized that he had ignored his own need to be loved fully in return by Doris. Memories of how they had related to each other in the past came flooding into his consciousness. He recalled how he would massage Doris for an hour while she would massage him for five minutes and then complain that she was too tired. Each time Ralph assured her that this was perfectly all right. He recalled how she never seemed to ask him for anything and that even after three years of marriage he did not know what she really liked or wanted. Ralph simply went about giving to her as best he could, using his own feelings and intuition about what she liked. Most of the ways he gave had been pleasing to Doris. The more he thought of it, the more he realized that he hadn't felt loved by Doris even though she had continuously told him how much she loved him. He had wants and needs which he had not been willing to express. For example, although he had always been the initiator of sex, he had kept hoping that she would approach him occasionally. Now he saw that his giving was not unconditional and that he had many expectations, however subtle they might be. He became aware that he had done things to please her while also hoping that she would be more active sexually as a result.

Finally the day of confrontation had come: "I know you love me but you don't act as if you do. I don't feel you want to give to me." Doris's response to this statement had been silence. She dismissed the whole thing as one of Ralph's fantasies. She had told him that he didn't know what he was talking about.

Ralph became increasingly aware that he was angry at feeling emotionally deprived by Doris. He was not the unconditional giver he thought he was. He began to make more requests in terms of his own needs. She in turn accused him of being demanding. He began to see how their relationship was a one-way street: he gave and she received. He realized that the main reason for his depression was his feeling of loneliness, a feeling of not being loved. In the months that followed, the confrontations became more frequent and more intense, Ralph insisting that unless the relationship became more gratifying to him, he was going to get a divorce.

Doris continued to dismiss such statements as a stage Ralph was going through. Since she knew how much Ralph loved her, she remained convinced that these were only words. One day, when she returned from shopping, there was a letter on the table. Ralph had packed his bags and left.

When we manipulate, we always end up being manipulated in return. Even the best intentions do not alter the destructive effect on manipulation on any relationship. Ralph finally came to terms with his own self-induced pattern of loneliness. He had been confused about his depression and had been unable to see it as a manifestation of loneliness. As is inevitably the case for each of us, Ralph's primary work was with himself. The best he could do was to share his feelings with Doris and, when no acknowledgment or resolution was forthcoming, to confront himself with a choice of holding onto an endlessly frustrating relationship or of breaking out. He chose to move on in search of something more gratifying and meaningful, and resolved to give up his "nice-guy" and "I-don't-need-anything" facades.

Most of us are aware that at times we simply feel like giving to someone, being with them, or responding to their needs. Usually with much more reluctance, we can become aware of our expectation of some kind of response in return.

Unconditional giving is not indiscriminate giving. Nourishing people do not pour their nourishment into relationships that are like bottomless pits. Needing nourishment from others is entirely different from expecting it. ("I deserve it"/"I have a right to it"/"You owe it to me.") In a one-way relationship, nourishing people will begin to lose interest and simply find themselves feeling less giving. Even then, they take responsibility for any resentment or disappointment they may feel, rather than get caught in any expectation about how the other person should be. They simply recognize the quality of the relationship and realize when they need something more. They are not interested in reprimanding, rebuking, or criticizing the person to whom they have been giving. Instead they confront themselves with the fact that whatever expectations they might have had are their own, and whatever frustration or rejection they feel must be resolved entirely within themselves.

Boredom

Boredom and loneliness tend to go hand in hand. When we feel lonely, our activities are often superficial distractions or meaningless drudgery. Boredom may be a general lethargy, an apathetic attitude toward life, or it may be manifested as a gnawing restlessness and discontent. It is as if we have an itch and don't know where to scratch.

WHEN WE FEEL LONELY WE ARE
USUALLY BORED WITH OURSELVES.

Boredom leads to loneliness and is a reflection of a lack of awareness of our inner potentials or our willingness to utilize them. Instead we prefer to wait, and expect the world to relieve us of our boredom (somebody turn me on!).

Bored and lonely people are usually unwilling to commit any energy and persistence to their efforts. Whenever we settle for what is immediately available, especially the kind of external stimulation that we can experience passively, we may actually be deadening our own potentials. In that sense we sow the seeds of future boredom. Our choice of action is usually limited to those choices which are most readily available or require the least effort to elicit gratification. One prime example of easy gratification is eating when we are not hungry, i.e., eating to escape boredom.

While immediate, relatively effortless gratifications, such as watching television, may be pleasurable, they can also become distractions which we use to avoid confronting ourselves with our boredom and taking full responsibility for it. We block our own ability to motivate ourselves enough to discover how to *create* meaningfulness in our lives.

To create meaningfulness, excitement, and joy which can provide real sustenance we must be actively involved. Involvement can, and often is, initially tedious and frustrating. When we have been lonely for some time we may have little tolerance for persevering in discovering and developing our interests if the initial progress is difficult. When we fail to see immediate results, we tend to lose heart, abandon the project, and move on to something else. Since our society offers a superabundance of passive, short-term turn-ons, this kind of avoidance can continue indefinitely. We can make the pursuit of external events into a life-style in which we incessantly flip to one after another. Yet we continue to find ourselves bored since, as each event ends and we remain unwilling to commit ourselves to discovering how to create our own meaningfulness, we are left with boredom.

Suicide

When we feel chronically lonely, suicidal thoughts are a common preoccupation. Since most of us have been strongly

indoctrinated with success-achievement myths, it is not diffi
cult to depress ourselves with fantasies about what we should
have accomplished, or to feel that our "failures" make life not
worth living. To make matters worse, we usually imagine that
others are "doing much better" and feel successful and happy.
Nowhere is the paralyzing power of judgments and comparisons
more clearly manifested than when severe loneliness culminates
in preoccupation with suicidal thoughts. The overwhelming
majority of lonely people who have either contemplated suicide
or actually made attempts are frightened and fearful of death.
When we fear death (which is not at all the same thing as not
wanting to die) we are often just as fearful of being fully alive.
Suicide is often the culmination of a fear of life. It is a dramatic
example of being stuck in the past, and in that sense is a
refusal to accept the fact that reality is experiencing life in the
constantly unfolding present. Instead, when we contemplate
suicide we are constantly contaminating the ongoing present
of our lives by clinging to past traumas and disappointments.
The tendency is to feel sure that the future will only be a
repetition of an unhappy past—or even worse. In this way, we
actually make our past into a *self-fulfilling* prophecy about our
future.

> SUICIDE IS A STATEMENT THAT WE
> WOULD RATHER DIE THAN BREAK OUT
> OF THE PAST.

Lost in our fantasies of failure and doom, we blind ourselves
to the present. We imagine that we are running out of time
and opportunities—or have already run out. We refuse to see
that when we choose to live in the present, each day is the
first day of the rest of our lives. This means breaking out of
what has been done and cannot be undone. It means getting on
with living in the present.

Almost everyone at times has had thoughts of suicide.
Suicide, when it is contemplated or attempted because of
loneliness, is a manifestation of overwhelming feelings of
helplessness, a statement of extreme impotence. It is, in effect,

an acknowledgment that we see no other real possibility of resolving the pain of our loneliness except death.

Lonely people who feel strongly suicidal are usually convinced that they have tried everything. Indeed, the range of their experimentation and efforts to help themselves is usually extensive. Often, they have tenaciously clung to the fantasy that there is a specific answer that could finally resolve their loneliness, but that it has somehow eluded them.

When Susan told Carl she was ending their relationship, his response was to threaten suicide. Carl was a chronically depressed, lonely man who always searched for someone he could lean on who would handle his fears and anxieties. In a way Susan was a worthy counterpart with her need to rescue other people. Being initially attracted to Carl it was easy for her to fall into the role of "Red Cross worker" and to make a rescue mission out of her relationship with him. She was well aware that she was suited to her career of nursing because it gave her the feeling of being needed.

From the beginning, Carl was quite open (though others would say he was dumping his emotional problems on Susan). He was thirty-two years old and had had suicidal thoughts since his early teens. He knew he was attractive to women and used women as a way of dealing with his chronic depression. He had considerable insight into his behavior but felt unable to use his insight. Suicidal thoughts became one of his ways of manipulating women. While he actually behaved like a helpless, incompetent child, his explanation was that he wanted to share every aspect of his life with someone he loved and who loved him.

Once again he pulled his trump card as he had successfully in the past with other women: the threat of suicide. He would systematically set about developing a new relationship so that it was always he who finally did the rejecting as he moved on to a new victim.

Susan was well prepared for Carl's reactions. She had thought about it a great deal. She hoped he would decide against attempting to end his life but realized she could not stop him without violating her own integrity. In any case, she insisted that this was the end of their relationship.

That night Susan got a call about three in the morning from Carl. He had swallowed whatever tranquilizers and sedatives were in his apartment. She called the police, who reached Carl in time. A few days later he was discharged from the hospital, despite his threat to kill himself at the first opportunity. Carl was angry and depressed because his suicidal ploy had not worked. He started psychotherapy and soon began to see that his ability to manipulate women led nowhere and he would have to give it up if he were ever to discover a more meaningful way of being and relating that might really resolve his loneliness. This was a very painful choice for Carl and one that took great courage. Gradually he began to feel his own strength emerging. It was a shock to him that he could stand the pain of his depression without having to dump it on any of the women who were available to listen. The more he worked within himself, the stronger he became, until eventually he reached the point at which he knew that his suicidal impulses and depression were not only manipulative but also manifested his deep fear of his inability to cope with the world on his own. Finally he was ready to break out of his loneliness.

6

~~~~~~~

How to Stop Playing
Self-Destructive
Loneliness Games

We have established by now that all attitudes and behavior patterns leading to chronic loneliness are self-induced and self-perpetuated. In each of us who has felt significantly lonely, a unique, self-induced constellation of these patterns operates. As long as we manifest these toxic attitudes and behavior patterns with sufficient intensity we will continue to perpetuate our loneliness. Whether we are aware of it or not, these patterns have a highly destructive effect on our overall well-being, literally draining our physical and emotional energy. They are particularly destructive when we are struggling to break out of loneliness. The persistence of these patterns is the principal factor in the evolution of loneliness into a chronic emotional state.

Patterns of loneliness always provide the comfort of the familiar and, regardless of how destructive they may be, they provide us with a sense of security and protection against real or imaginary threats.

We human beings are ingenious creatures and when we feel chronically lonely, we devise a whole repertoire of patterns, our particular brand of a vicious cycle which only returns us to the endless anxiety and emotional pain of our loneliness. The larger our repertoire, the easier it is to continue to avoid our awareness of the futility of our actions. We create more confusion by adding an unrealistic complexity to our lives which blinds us all the more and makes the resolution of our loneliness even more remote. The more we complicate our lives, the greater the likelihood that we will remain confused and lost in the maze of our mental ruminations and dead-end pursuits, which we ourselves have created.

WHEN WE ARE LONELY WE SELDOM ADD ANYTHING NEW TO OUR EXISTENCE.

Often what appears to be new is only a different variation of the same old pattern. For example, we may bring new people into our lives and delude ourselves that we are doing something about our loneliness because we now have more friends. If we cling to the same self-defeating attitudes and behavior patterns and allow these to continue to dictate how we function with new relationships, the outcome will be the same.

We may sincerely believe that we are relating in a new, more nourishing fashion. Common sense might suggest that when our persistent "new" attempts repeatedly fail perhaps we are missing something basic in our whole approach. This awareness seldom occurs, even though our loneliness continues to deepen and our feelings of futility and hopelessness continue to grow.

Games include any kind of behavior intended to manipulate or pressure ourselves or others. *All* games are toxic. Game-playing is an unnatural behavior, in that it lacks both spontaneity and honesty. All of us play games at times. When we are lonely it is important to become aware of how these games directly affect our loneliness. Then it is our responsibility to decide whether or not we wish to continue to play them.

Behavior patterns of self-induced loneliness represent a particular kind of game. They are manipulations and/or excuses to avoid the threat of open, authentic relating both inwardly and toward others. Games of loneliness are those manipulations of ourselves or others, those patterns of attitudes and behavior that ultimately lead to feelings of isolation and alienation.

Since loneliness is a universal experience, all of us can

identify with some or all of these patterns to some degree. In this respect, a nourishing response to patterns of loneliness is to become more aware of their existence and their destructive effect on our lives. The resolution of loneliness begins with the development of awareness of what our patterns are and how these attitudes and behaviors actually generate our loneliness.

Toxic Initiating

When caught up in the pain of loneliness, we may fail to see that our way of initiating contact is often inappropriate and therefore almost certain to be ineffective.

When John enrolled in a large university in a strange city, his chronic loneliness quickly reached a peak of desperation. In an attempt to make friends he began driving around campus picking up hitchhiking students. He said he was going whichever way they were going. He would start conversations but was usually met with nonchalant responses from his rider. Time after time he avoided facing this lack of response and continued his manipulations. He would be convinced he was really starting a friendship as he continued to initiate superficial conversation. These dialogues became more difficult to sustain on longer trips. He worked harder to keep them going, while his rider usually became less and less responsive. The climax of John's game occurred when his rider was about to get out of the car and thanked him. He would then say something to the effect of: "How about having a cup of coffee together sometime?" His invitation invariably met with a cliché response and nothing more ever came of it.

A similar example is Elaine, a lonely widow in her midforties whose husband left her financially well off. She ate out almost every evening and made it a point to frequent the same restaurants so that the employees came to know her. She deliberately arrived early when few customers were around and she tipped extremely well. While the employees were usually friendly and occasionally mentioned something to her about themselves and their personal lives, no real friendships developed. Her well-intended efforts to make friends were totally ineffective.

In the cases of John and Elaine, superficial contact under specific circumstances that dominate the interaction is confused with a more appropriate means by which to relate to someone new. Both took advantage of a captive audience so that the mutual spontaneity of a naturally developing relationship was aborted.

Marilyn's constant complaint was: "Why does every man I become interested in turn out to be married?" Marilyn was not only lonely but also fed up with the way the men she dated deceived her. She was unaware of her subtle ways of initiating these relationships and her encouragement of married men. She assumed that "any decent man" who was married would not approach her or would reject any approach of hers. Obviously, she also assumed that she could only be attracted to "decent" men in the first place.

As each affair ended and plunged her back into loneliness, she resolved to avoid any future involvement with married men, yet her relationships continued to be remarkably similar. When an interesting man would ask her out, she failed to do the obvious and ask if he was married. When she eventually discovered that he was married, she would find an excuse to continue, while rationalizing that she could "keep it light," but she persistently avoided confronting herself with her intense involvement. On other occasions, after her lover disclosed that he was married, Marilyn's response was largely anger at him for "spoiling the relationship."

In therapy her pattern became clearer to her as she became more fully aware of her intense fear of deep involvement in a long-term relationship with its subsequent threat of rejection. Her brief affairs avoided what she perceived to be the overwhelming catastrophe of rejection after a prolonged relationship. She eventually understood that this was also the principal reason she had turned down several marriage proposals in the past.

Her toxic initiating paid off with inevitable rejection. While she felt considerable love for some of these men, the brevity of her affairs limited her involvement and hurt. Eventually she realized that subconsciously she knew all along that her lovers were married and that they lied. Thus Marilyn created a life-style in which she endured long periods of loneliness but protected herself from the intolerable devastation of rejection after a prolonged relationship. She now understood that by being involved with a married man she could precipitate a crisis in each relationship before her emotional involvement had become so intense that a breakup would be too painful.

Like Marilyn, the chronically lonely are often unaware of whom they choose to become involved with. Typically, they initiate relationships with people who are more readily available for superficial relationships (including affairs) than for long-term intimacies, thereby avoiding their fear of intimacy and their fear of rejection, both of which may intensify as an intimate relationship deepens and shows possibilities of enduring.

> BECAUSE OF THE DESPERATION WE
> FEEL WHEN WE ARE DEEPLY LONELY,
> WE MAY DEVELOP INTIMACY WITH
> OTHERS, EVEN THOUGH WE ALREADY
> KNOW THAT THE SUBSEQUENT
> RELATIONSHIPS WON'T BE
> SATISFACTORY.

With this destructive initiation, the relationship is apt to continue only as long as our desperation remains. Then our discrimination returns and the relationship begins to deteriorate.

The Rescuers

The rescuer frequently steps into the void created by the pain of loneliness, which leads them into relationships with others whom they know can't fulfill their needs. Rescuers choose to relate to those people who are obviously in desperate need and their availability is almost certain to insure that the fear of rejection is practically nil. We may in good faith see ourselves as rescuers of seriously depressed people and set about trying to break them out of their loneliness. In so doing, we make ourselves willing victims on whom they can dump depression. When we choose to become rescuers we are usually convinced that not only are we able to tolerate their depression (which is possible), but in addition that we can "save" the other person from it (which is extremely unlikely). As rescuers, we usually sense but won't confront ourselves with the fact that the relationship is sustained because we fulfill this desperate need. There is no giving in this pattern since, in essence, it is a way for each to use the other.

Rescuers avoid the inner confrontation that could lead to awareness of the futility of the relationship. Instead, we, as rescuers, cling to our belief that we are helping the person to resolve their unhappiness. The manipulative aspect of lonely rescuers is the hidden expectation of receiving the other person's undying gratitude once the rescue succeeds, thereby insuring a stable and lasting relationship and an end to loneliness.

The lonely rescuer often plays this role for a considerable period of time.

Knowlin was a painfully shy man of thirty-five whose self-image centered on his premature baldness. He was so self-conscious about it that he concluded no woman could possibly find him attractive. He would not wear a hairpiece out of fear that when a woman discovered his baldness, she not only would reject him but would in addition accuse him of being a phony.

Knowlin felt that the best way to escape his unbearable loneliness was to become economically secure and then find a financially needy woman—hopefully a desperate one. For years he had worked two full-time jobs, living very meagerly, while investing in real estate with his savings. These investments were very profitable and he became a wealthy man. He bought a large home, furnished it elaborately, and was ready to make his move to find a woman who was insecure, preferably not too attractive, and ideally with at least two children to support. He hoped she would also have minimal skills with which to earn a living. Knowlin reasoned that because of her circumstances, she would be willing to tolerate his baldness and the other inadequacies he felt so deeply. He would rescue her from poverty and, in turn, would have a safe relationship based on her desperation. He hoped to resolve his loneliness once and for all.

He congratulated himself that his plan was going to pay off when he met Ursula. Ursula's husband had been killed in a car accident two years earlier. She had three children and had managed to support them by moving in with her parents and working as a salesperson in a large department store. She was forty, slightly overweight, and also seemed quite lonely. Knowlin decided she would fit his requirements perfectly, and he began dating her and helping her financially; a few months later he proposed marriage.

Ursula was very much in love with Knowlin. Caught up in his own self-poisoning game of rescuer, he could not believe this and was convinced that she had accepted his proposal because of his money and the material things he promised.

It wasn't long before she began to feel that her love was not reciprocated. When she confronted him, he pointed out the home and economic security as expressions of his love. She tried in vain to convince him that she never would have married him for his money. Two years later Ursula left him, returned to her old job, and moved back to her parents' home.

Passive Relating

When we feel too threatened about initiating relationships or investing ourselves emotionally, to the extent that we are vulnerable to the pain of possible rejection we may limit our relationships to those that others initiate and sustain single-handedly. In essence, we respond to these overtures passively and accept the relationship largely because of the interest of others, who are clearly available to us, rather than because we reciprocate their feelings.

> Loraine worked as a receptionist for a men's clothing manufacturer, greeting buyers from all parts of the country who came to the showroom, many of them several times a year. She dated some regularly when they were in town. Usually it was dinner or the theater and occasionally a weekend together. While she enjoyed the attention of so many interesting men, and indeed had a full social life, she felt depressed and lonely because of the sporadic nature of these relationships. Some of these men she grew to care for a great deal. Almost all of them were married, but she never concerned herself with this. "After all, these relationships aren't going anyplace," she would tell herself.
>
> Actually Loraine wanted a more enduring and intimate relationship. She kept telling herself she should stop dating out-of-towners and look for a relationship that might have a future to it, meanwhile settling for what was most available. In so doing she was actually unavailable for dates with men from her own community. She frequently refused dates with local men because she was busy with her out-of-town friends.

The Professional Psychologizer

Understanding and psychological insight are easily distorted into tools for stalemating one's self. Entangling ourselves in a maze of analysis of every nuance of our own psyche and others as well can become a destructive pattern. Amateur psychological intellectualizing can be endless and often becomes nothing more than a combination of sophisticated nit-picking and subtle manifestations of hostility; e.g., interpreting someone else's behavior for them, whether they like it or not. The value of such intellectual "insight" is, to say the least, often grossly exaggerated and is certainly not a prerequisite to the active experimentation and risk-taking needed to discover how to break out of our loneliness. Rather "insight" easily becomes an excuse to avoid living our lives in the present. We can use our interpretations, explanations, and "answers" as excuses to avoid the true issues behind our loneliness.

> PSYCHOLOGIZING IS A DEFINITE
> HINDRANCE TO BREAKING OUT OF
> CHRONIC LONELINESS.

This form of so-called intellectual understanding and explanation serves primarily as a barrier against constructive action which leads to breaking out of our loneliness.

Lonely people who victimize themselves with this pattern often enjoy telling their life story to anyone who will listen, seeming to take satisfaction in recounting in detail their past tragedies, rejections, and misfortunes. With considerable psychological sophistication, they explain their personality. These intellectual discourses are impressive and often valid; however, they are used primarily to justify loneliness. "Understanding" becomes a self-perpetuating pattern that only leads to more loneliness and is most apt to be used to avoid actual risk-taking and experimentation.

> Phillip had been to four different therapists over a ten-year period. He had attended numerous workshops, encounter groups, and other organized approaches to personal growth, hoping to find a way of alleviating his loneliness. At thirty, in addition to his considerable experience in psychotherapy, he had a bachelor's degree in psychology.
>
> In therapy he consistently intellectualized his problems and avoided any emotional involvement. When his therapist pointed this out, his response was a sophisticated explanation of this "resistance" or, as he often put it: "the unresolved roots of my neurosis." He managed to distort the purpose of his therapy and incorporate it into his pattern of self-induced loneliness by intellectualizing the whole process. Any new insights or understanding

he gained were used to create new ways of avoiding the ultimate confrontation with himself and those self-destructive patterns so rampant in his attitudes toward himself and in his personal relationships.

He always insisted that the primary solution to his loneliness depended on intimate involvements with women. His relations with women varied from intense one-to-one commitments to multiple relationships, including group sex. Women were drawn to him because of his intellectual ability and his apparent openness in sharing himself with them. However, his sharing was purely intellectual and a mere repetition of the psychological understanding and explanations which he could recite by rote. He continued to limit his relations to the safety of his role as an habitual psychologizer, a part he played skillfully, often intellectualizing about other people's problems and making astute interpretations. This only enhanced the intellectual quality of his relating and was his safeguard against risking any real intimacy or openness. The more he related in this manner, the more intense his loneliness became. Surprisingly he had no insight into this pattern. When people suggested that his psychologizing turned them off, he interpreted this as their "defensiveness against the truth" (which only turned them off more).

His standard psychological explanation of his emotional difficulties began with the recitation of his childhood traumas. He talked about the insensitivity and unavailability of his parents and how this affected his feelings of security and acceptance. He developed these explanations with elaborate examples of specific traumatic experiences designed to arouse the empathy of his listener. He often manipulated women into trying to provide him with the acceptance and love he had convinced them he never had.

When he drank excessively, he took on a self-pitying attitude. Those women who felt moved by his "openness" and attempted to reassure him soon discovered that he always had a sophisticated psychological explanation (excuse) about how difficult it was for him to believe anyone could accept him. In this way he drained the energies of each woman he became involved with, and they became aware of the futility of their efforts and their own growing feelings of emotional exhaustion. Phillip had learned to use his intellect and his psychological sophistication to suck the love and energy from other people. While at times he felt some temporary relief from his loneliness, he gradually became more deeply lonely as each relationship ended and he had to renew his search for someone with whom to start his game again.

It was during a weekend encounter group that he met Sylvia, a vivacious woman who was more than a match for his intellectual games. She refused to be suckered by his line and avoided being manipulated by his psychological skills, his intellectualizing, or his self-pity.

Phillip was aware of his growing involvement with Sylvia and felt increasingly frustrated by his inability to pull love from her in his usual manipulative fashion. They became more blunt: "Don't dump your psychology stuff on me," she told him when he started playing games.

Gradually Phillip felt a growing trust toward Sylvia and began to let go of his psychologizing. He became increasingly aware of how effective his games were in avoiding intimacy and its feared subsequent rejection. As he became more open, Sylvia became more loving and giving. When he reverted to his old patterns, she continued to resist. As he continued to grow more open and honest, his love and trust for Sylvia increased and the manipulative patterns with which he had created his loneliness faded into the background. For the first time in his life, Phillip experienced the joy of a nourishing relationship that continued to grow.

Phillip's case illustrates how we can discover a way to break out of the endless repetition of patterns of self-induced loneliness. While Sylvia's ability to relate to Phillip in an open, authentic manner foiled him in his manipulative games, the critical issue remained in Phillip's hands. This time he chose to respond more honestly.

While it always takes two to play any manipulative game, none of us can resolve the loneliness of another person, no matter how much love or caring we invest. In the final analysis, breaking out of loneliness must be accomplished through inner confrontations with one's self and a willingness to experiment with different kinds of behavior.

The Idealized Image

Many people live dominated by an idealized image of themselves, i.e., their personal fantasy of how they should be, look, or behave and the various self-imposed rules and goals they believe they must live up to.

OUR IDEALIZED IMAGE IS OUR CURSE.

It must be seen as a powerful impediment to accepting and loving our self *as we are* and to experiencing intimacy with ourselves and others. The attitudes and behavior patterns dictated by our idealized image reflect the expectations that we imagine must be met in order for use to be acceptable. These goals are always unattainable to a satisfactory degree, as they place unrealistic demands on us in the first place.

For example, many of us are dominated by an idealized image that demands we be gregarious, poised, or even-tempered, regardless of our mood. We may behave in a stereotypical manner, responding appropriately and rarely venturing to say or do anything controversial or self-revealing. Or, we may make it a point to always appear pleasant and genuinely interested in everyone. Often our image demands that we keep up with current events, books, or whatever, regardless of our interest or lack of it. Since openness is a threat, our idealized image becomes a wall which defends us from other people.

The inner world of the chronically lonely who are trapped by their idealized image is filled with anxiety about presenting the "right" picture. They are usually obsessed with what others think about them, or they constantly analyze themselves. After most social encounters, they torture themselves by ruminating about possible goofs they may have made, or stew for days out of fear that something they said or did might have annoyed someone.

Sometimes, in an effort to conceal our shame and embarrassment about being lonely, we present an image of being without fear or anxiety. We may take on an air of bravado, an "I don't give a damn" attitude. The self-poisoning aspect of this pattern usually centers on an idealized image we project, and may now feel stuck with—that we aren't supposed to need anyone. Breaking out of this phony image of self-sufficiency and showing our real self becomes increasingly difficult. Old phobias about being unlovable or unacceptable continue to intensify as long as we hide behind these protective facades. Our fear that others might see beneath the surface inevitably limits our likelihood of experiencing real intimacy.

> TRYING TO SUSTAIN OUR IDEALIZED
> IMAGE IS AN ENDLESS TASK BLOCKING
> THE WAY TOWARD DISCOVERING THE
> GREATER DEPTH AND
> MEANINGFULNESS THAT EXISTS
> WITHIN EACH OF US.

You First

One of the most obvious games played to avoid the risk of rejection is to passively wait for others not only to initiate the relationship but to continue in this role indefinitely. When the other person must continuously "go first," we passively control the relationship. The essence of the "you first" game is: "Here I am. You must approach me, *then* maybe I'll respond." Since fear of rejection is so widespread, we are apt to come into contact with others who have the same fears. The potential for meaningful relationships is aborted when each of us holds back and avoids contact. Ironically, in this way, many of us enhance our mutual loneliness. It is quite common for two people who are interested in each other to hold back out of fear of being rejected, therefore quietly forfeiting the intimacy that is there for the taking.

The cause of the "you first" game is the fear of not being lovable. Most people, even in this day of apparent psychological enlightenment, still fear that exploring their deeper selves will lead to their discovering thoughts, feelings, or impulses that will confirm the dreaded fear that they are indeed unlovable. This deep-seated phobia may remain throughout their entire lives, threatening to burst forth if probed too much. Another aspect of this same fantasy takes the form of a chronic anxiety that, were we to open ourselves to intimacy, others would discover these same hidden horrors and instantly terminate the relationship.

All of us have feelings or memories about which we feel a sense of shame or guilt. In developing an open, trusting relationship, the sharing of these "unacceptable" aspects is one of the most powerful (and frightening) ways of deepening and strengthening intimacy. Those who play the "you first" game are particularly emphatic in their ground rules when it comes to openness. Not only does the other person have to go first in "exposing" himself or herself, but in addition the lonely person must feel assured that whatever he or she "exposes" in return is revealed to a much lesser degree, in order to feel assured that the other person remains more vulnerable. Sometimes the other person must clearly be more deeply involved, "in love." This protective "advantage" (I can hurt you more than you can hurt me!) is persistently maintained throughout the relationship. The self-induced loneliness generated through this game is further exacerbated by the fact that the lonely person is limited to relating to those who seem more insecure or more vulnerable.

Cocktail Party Relationships

Many gregarious people seem to be submerged in a superabundance of relationships, yet are emotionally and psychologically isolated. Their interaction is characteristically superficial and marked by an absence of real emotional contact. There is little genuine excitement or enthusiasm in their relationships, which may remain on the same superficial level, often for years, while their loneliness is rampant. These relationships are often based on activities or interests which people participate in together. For example, co-workers, business contacts, or members of the same club, church, or other organizations have "friends" who are usually readily interchangeable, which is a manifestation of their lack of intimate relating. Activity per se, whether business or pleasure, is often their primary motivation. In contrast is the often-portrayed picture of two lovers walking hand in hand. While they may be going no place special and talking very little, one feels their closeness. The intimacy they share is so overwhelming that verbal exchange or the pursuit of activities they enjoy together is obviously of secondary importance.

Quantity is never a substitute for quality when it comes to meaningful relating. The number of relationships any of us has is scarcely relevant. We may be perplexed about why we are lonely when we have so many friends and an active social life. We may be deluged with invitations, participate in numerous activities, yet at the same time feel bored and isolated. In such instances it is likely that we have overloaded ourselves with "cocktail party" encounters. The conversations are largely trite and filled with platitudes and clichés or, while interesting or stimulating, remain impersonal and center on discussions of politics, world affairs, sports, and other subjects of this nature.

"I don't know why I'm lonely. I've got a whole phonebook of people I can call, and I'm busy all the time."

This was Larry's comment as he felt increasingly perplexed by a sudden realization that despite constant parties and dating, he continually felt lonely and depressed. His initial attempt to find a solution was to increase his "body count": the number of people he could call or spend time with so that he need not be alone. For Larry being alone *was* being lonely. In launching his new campaign, he increased the frequency and variety of his activities.

He had a date for lunch each day and filled every evening with activities with different people. On weekends he took on still more activities and surrounded himself with as many people as possible. Yet his loneliness only intensified, as did his desperation. He was convinced that more is better, that by filling his life with more people and activities he would ultimately be living such a full life that there would be no time for loneliness. Larry was unaware that all his well-meant efforts only further diminished the quality of his intimacy, thereby perpetuating and intensifying his loneliness.

After some months of this well-meant program he was physically exhausted, to the point where he couldn't bring himself to get out of bed and he would sleep through most of the weekend. He had created a life-style in which he was constantly on the run without experiencing any gratification in what he was doing. He hoped that eventually he would get used to his busy routine and that his life-style would resolve his loneliness. Meanwhile, his behavior was becoming increasingly stereotyped and automatic. His "program" was actually "running" him.

Despite his growing fatigue, it became increasingly difficult to sleep. He would awaken in the middle of the night, sweating profusely and filled with anxiety. He felt as if he had had bad dreams which he could not remember. Lying awake in the early hours of the morning, he felt his loneliness surge up more intensely than ever and he began to have suicidal thoughts.

A complete physical checkup was negative. When his physician suggested psychotherapy, he felt resentful.

"I'm not crazy. Why do you want me to see a 'shrink'? My problem is that I can't sleep well."

Larry was totally unwilling to accept the possibility that his insomnia was a manifestation of his loneliness. Quite to the contrary, he considered his insomnia as an interference with the program of activities that he continued to insist would eventually end his loneliness. He persisted in following his rigorous schedule and a few months later had developed an ulcer. Reluctantly, he agreed to try psychotherapy.

During one session his therapist asked him to role-play, talking to himself while looking into a mirror, and to simply say the words: "Larry, I love you." To his utter amazement, he was unable to express this simple statement. It just wouldn't come out. Painful as this was, it opened the door to a new awareness of how he was perpetuating his loneliness. He had always been afraid to look inward for fear of what he might discover, although he had no idea what that might be.

As he began to explore his inner self, he became more loving, more intimate, and more caring toward himself. Now, for the first time since he could remember, he began to enjoy solitude.

His new inner attitude radiated out to other people. He gave up his rat race of activities and became more selective about the people he related to. He actually began to enjoy others and to appreciate them as individuals. Some friends he had known for years, he now realized, he did not know at all. Having been so preoccupied with his loneliness, he had been blindly unaware of others. His focus had always been directed toward trying to manipulate himself and everyone around him so that he could escape his loneliness. Now, with his sharing, open attitude, his loneliness began to melt away.

Larry had found a resolution to loneliness which turned him in a different direction; one that he had never dared to explore. He saw the futility of what he now called "the poison of going and doing." It was a few months later that he met Laura. His new sensitivity and awareness enabled him to be more open, sharing, and responsive to her. He experienced the most meaningful relationship of his life with Laura. In his last therapy session he announced that they were to be married and that he felt as if he had been reborn.

Larry's resolution of his loneliness exemplifies how, with greater awareness, any of us can discover the way we continue a life-style that creates chronic loneliness. When Larry was willing to risk exploring his inner self, he found that everything he needed to make his life fulfilling and meaningful had existed within him all the time but was meaningless as long as it remained undiscovered.

7

~~~~~~~~

How to Stop Setting Traps for Yourself

Each of us can develop a pattern of self-induced loneliness that can become so much a part of our attitudes and life-style that it may not even occur to us to question it. Becoming aware of these negative patterns opens the door to the exploration and discovery of new dimensions of living, new attitudes and ways of relating to ourselves and to the world, which can be far more nourishing and can lead to an effective resolution of our loneliness.

The Ostrich Syndrome

When there is something happening in our lives that we do not want to face up to, we may choose to play ostrich, so that what we don't see won't threaten us. We may even convince ourselves, at least temporarily, that whatever concerned us no longer exists. Typically the player of the ostrich game is convinced that an intimate relationship with a loving person would resolve his or her loneliness, and the player refuses to see any established patterns of self-induced loneliness. Figuratively speaking, we may stick our heads in the sand about our manipulation of others, our playing of phony games, and especially our desire to avoid focusing on our own lack of inner intimacy and self-love. Similarly, we may try to be unaware of our need to avoid confronting ourselves with what-

79

ever fears or anxieties we feel block us from effectively developing intimacy. When we play ostrich, we literally don't want to see anything that might threaten our existing relationships. We don't want to see the warning signs that would tell us our intimate relationships are heading for trouble. The ostrich attitude goes like this: "Don't confuse me with facts, my mind is made up. Everything is all right and I don't want any serious problems."

When Marianne met David he seemed to be an open, warm person. He was a good listener and his responsiveness made Marianne feel he really understood her. "I feel that way too," was his frequent response when she would reveal to him something about herself that was intimate or important. She chose not to pay attention to his fidgeting while she was sharing her deep, intimate feelings with him.

After they were married, David's anxieties and desire to avoid intimate sharing become too obvious for Marianne to avoid any longer. She began to feel that he was trying to play a role and give the responses he knew she wanted, while hoping that each such encounter would end quickly. She realized that he had reacted this way from the beginning. She knew that before their marriage she hadn't wanted to see this; that she had ignored this and anything else she feared might cause a conflict between them. She had been lonely for a long time and desperately wanted to find someone she could love. Marriage to David seemed the resolution to her loneliness.

It was only a matter of months before he burst forth in an angry tirade: "You don't want a husband, you want a confidant. Why can't we just go about our own business and live together? Why do you always have to move in on me with your problems and fears? I can't stand this constant closeness and your expecting me to always be so agreeable and understanding." David stormed out of the room while Marianne sat in stunned disbelief. She had married a person whose idea of intimacy was the exact opposite of hers. It became clear to her that David wanted a more superficial relationship—"a practical marriage" as he later put it.

It was painful when Marianne realized that she had married David not to find intimacy, as she had convinced herself at the time, but rather to avoid intimacy and *her* fear of it. Now she could clearly see that from the very beginning David had always wanted to close her off. He provided a protection for her against her own anxieties about self-disclosure and vulnerability. She had felt safe with him because his anxiety about intimacy was even more intense and more quickly mobilized than her own. He aborted their exchanges before she even felt threatened by her own fear of intimacy.

All patterns of self-induced loneliness are manifestations of some form of manipulation of one's self and/or others. Manipulation is often referred to as a "game" since there are various rules, almost always unspoken and often unconscious, that dominate the attitudes and behavior of the game player and determine the pattern of his or her ways of relating both inwardly and to others. Referring to the pattern as a "game" does not in any way imply that it is a trivial aspect of living. On the contrary, games of self-induced loneliness are emotionally highly toxic and often have a disastrous effect on one's well-being.

Marianne played the ostrich game very well. She found a willing partner in David, who was also lonely but consciously aware of wanting to avoid an intimate relationship. Each played out the game until the inevitable occurred. Game playing does not provide the emotional nourishment each of us needs if we are to sustain and enhance an intimate relationship.

IT IS ONLY WHEN WE LEARN FROM
OUR OWN EXPERIENCE THAT GAMES
DON'T WORK THAT WE ARE READY TO
GIVE THEM UP.

When we pay attention, we can see quite early in any relationship the clues that point to those aspects that are apt to cause difficulties if the appropriate confrontations are avoided. When we are lonely and longing to develop a nourishing relationship with someone new who seems like "the right one" and are willing to risk paying attention and sharing these possibly troublesome areas, that is, when we are willing to let go of our ostrich games, the possibilities for a nourishing relationship are enormously enhanced.

> THERE ARE ALWAYS DIFFICULTIES IN
> ANY RELATIONSHIP. BURYING THEM IS
> NOT ONLY FUTILE BUT ACTUALLY
> ENHANCES THEIR POWER SO THAT
> ULTIMATELY THEY WILL BURST
> FORTH IN A FAR MORE DESTRUCTIVE
> FASHION.   ·

Face-to-face dialogues between people who are willing to express their differences, their anxieties, and so forth *without* waiting until such confrontations become a crisis can be a most effective prophylaxis against the subtle emergence of a toxic relationship. Compromises necessary in all relationships are much more likely to be discovered when they are dealt with continually. Sweeping them under the carpet, even with a sincere intent to face them later, makes discovery much less likely.

Marianne and David made a mutual acknowledgment that they both had deep fears of intimacy and self-disclosure. After the initial crisis, which included three brief separations over a six-month period, they finally began to talk about their difficulties. Such dialogues are a process, an ongoing aspect of any relationship.

> RELATIONSHIPS ARE NEVER STATIC;
> THEY ARE ALWAYS IN FLUX. WE DO
> NOT NEED TO FINISH WITH OUR
> DISCORDS IN ORDER TO HAVE A
> STABLE, GROWING RELATIONSHIP. WE
> DO NEED TO FACE THEM WITH LOVE
> AND MUTUAL CARING.

Both Marianne and David gradually became more trusting of themselves and each other. The initially stormy period of their marriage gradually evolved into a mutual trust that neither had ever thought possible. Now they can laugh about the "bumpy road" they traveled together in their marriage, *and* they have become wise enough to know how important it is to continue to be aware of each other's needs.

Narcissism

The desperation that often comes with chronic loneliness may cause us to become confused about the difference between self-love, a necessary prerequisite to intimacy with others, and various kinds of narcissistic attitudes and behavior. Narcissism implies that we are not concerned about how our actions affect others. "I'm going to let it all hang out; and it you don't like it, drop dead."

We have said that nourishing people are more open, self-expressive, and willing to risk rejection. However, this attitude can easily be distorted into a toxic I don't-give-a-damn attitude that ultimately leads to deep loneliness. While each of us is the center of our existence, we can use this as a license to ignore the needs and reactions of other people with whom we wish to relate or who are affected by our actions. Loneliness and emotional isolation are the fruits that come from alienating others. When we foster an ungiving, unloving atmosphere, this is most likely what we will get in return.

Insofar as our inner intimacy is concerned, narcissism usually becomes a pattern of impulsive self-indulgence. We give in to various whims while ignoring the fact that we are responsible for the consequences of our own acts. This is not a moral judgment but a fact of life. Responsibility is the ability to respond—in this case to ourselves. Our behavior *does* have an effect on our subsequent well-being, or the lack of it.

> "If people can't accept me because I'm fat, then I don't want to have anything to do with them. My weight is part of me and if someone is sexually turned-off because I'm fat, then that's just too damn bad."

This was Marty's angry response to the comment of

another group therapy member that physical appearance is one of the first things people react to when they initially meet. Marty had complained about his lack of dates while insisting that women didn't give themselves a chance to know him. Several women in the group agreed that while he had many attractive qualities, his weight made him sexually unattractive.

Dottie responded to Marty's angry defense by asking how he would feel about asking her for a date if she hadn't bathed for two weeks. Finally, Marty himself had to laugh after he tried to insist that a bad body odor would not make any real difference in how he felt about a woman. In that brief moment of insight Marty began to break out of his defensive and narcissistic attitude about his weight.

Gordon, on the other hand, was quick to side with Marty. He too felt that overweight shouldn't make any difference. Indeed, he knew women who preferred big men. After he spoke, someone else commented to Gordon that the dark glasses he constantly wore kept others from seeing his eyes and was, for her, another kind of turn-off. Like Marty, Gordon responded with defiance: "I like wearing dark glasses. I wear them all the time and I'll be damned if I'm going to take them off to please somebody else. If it turns you off, that's just too damned bad."

These narcissistic patterns are manifested in many subtle ways which consistently reveal a lack of awareness or concern about how they affect others. The other side of this coin is that narcissistic people are usually adamant that others relate to them according to their own expectations. Being disinterested in others and insensitive to how they react to us is an obvious pathway to loneliness.

Narcissistic personalities expect that changes toward more nourishing behavior should be noticed and acknowledged by others, an expectation which reflects a continuing narcissism even during an evolution toward less total self-centeredness.

The Paralysis of Disappointment

A prolonged state of chronic loneliness gradually erodes our ability to tolerate the inevitable disappointments of life and still continue to strive for what we want. We may convince ourselves that one more rejection or one more failure will be too much. This attitude easily results in a loss of interest in everyone and everything. Such overwhelming feelings of futility and paralysis are characteristic of deep depression. However, we can understand this pattern better when we recognize that it reflects a critical state of loneliness so overwhelmingly powerful that we may feel nothing can be done about it.

Most of us have never been taught to cope with the pain and frustration of disappointment. Parents often lead their children to believe that disappointment is an acceptable excuse to give up. They may even try to console their children by implying that disappointments are not supposed to happen. They may, out of love, try to spare their children from such experiences but, in so doing, they hamper their ability to learn to tolerate this inevitable aspect of living.

When we are lonely, we tend to see ourselves as vulnerable, as if the pain of loneliness has automatically weakened our stamina until we feel unable to strive for what we want. We may allow disappointment to wipe us out, as if we had run into a concrete wall which can neither be overcome nor circumvented. We behave as if our basic inner source of energy and motivation has been lost. The more self-nourishing we are, the more we can transmute the energy wasted in feeling futile and paralyzed into a more determined effort to get what we need.

When we give in to disappointments, our efforts toward making our lives more meaningful lessen. We tend to make half-hearted attempts, which, in turn, enhance the likelihood of more disappointment. It becomes easier to lapse into lethargy and futility, resulting in a further loss of our enthusiasm for living. Like so many patterns of chronic loneliness, this becomes a vicious cycle leading to deeper despair.

The reasons for our loneliness are easily blamed on other people or circumstances. Clinging to the fantasy that the outside world has let us down may provide a rationalization for our disappointments, but it only traps us more deeply in our loneliness. We safely avoid the essential confrontation with the truth: that we are the source of our discontent and have disappointed ourselves. Projection simply provides a different and convenient focus for blame and avoids responsibility. Such blaming games are a vicious cycle, to which there is no end unless we ourselves put an end to them.

The Mañana Syndrome

Criticism and perfectionism, when directed inward, readily turn into chronic self-rejection which, in turn, fosters chronic loneliness. We decide that we are not lovable until our "faults" are remedied.

Perfectionism results in a continuous failure to live our lives in the present and to do the best we can. Since there is no such thing as human perfection, our conclusion is that nothing we do is okay. As long as we cling to this kind of fantasy, we assure ourselves of continued loneliness, for this game is a refusal to live with and love (not necessarily like) our imperfections—simply because they are a part of us.

THE REFUSAL TO LIVE WITH OUR
FAULTS IS TANTAMOUNT TO A
REFUSAL TO LIVE AT ALL.

Instead we all too often choose to remain stuck. Of course, we apply the same relentless criticism and perfectionism used on ourselves to others and either openly or silently we demand the same flawless performance from them that we demand of ourselves. In short, we wait for the world to shape up and *then* we will start living. What better way is there to guarantee loneliness!

Procrastination is the refusal to live in the present. Life becomes a series of postponements.

Most procrastinators sincerely believe that one day they will begin a function actively once they resolve their imperfections. This attitude is similar to "New Year's resolutions." Despite the sincere intent, the sustained power necessary for growth and change is lacking. The growth process is erratic. At times we feel we are progressing, while at other times we feel static or regressive. Lack of progress is intolerable to the perfectionist and a "what's-the-use" attitude results. The lonely procrastinator who will not let go of the need for perfection usually fantasizes that he or she should show a steady, consistent progress.

Cal was a bright, sensitive boy who was the only child of two perfectionists. He had always felt he was lacking in some vital quality and was unacceptable and unlovable. In the face of constant criticism from his parents, he repeatedly resolved to do better. He conscientiously strove to improve and, most of all, not to repeat the same mistakes which angered his parents. Their principal obsession was that he excel in school. He became a straight A student but, to his dismay, his parents then focused their criticism on his personal grooming, his room, his unacceptable friends, and, sooner or later, practically every aspect of his life.

By the time he started high school, he had internalized these demands to the point where his self-criticism far exceeded his parents'. For example, he disqualified himself from any social life because of a slight case of acne. He remained shy and withdrawn and consistently rejected any gestures of friendship. By the time he began college, his acne had cleared and he then became overly critical of his body. He was a tall, lanky young man and some of his acquaintances nicknamed him "string bean." There were several women who found him attractive and told him so, but such comments were rejected as insincere gestures of kindness. He lifted weights and developed an outstanding physique. Still his self-criticism remained as harsh as ever.

Success in his career became his obsession until he was about forty. Most people who knew Cal had a great appreciation for him. He was a bright, handsome, successful man, yet he continued to isolate himself. His perfectionism had not waned in the least. As he approached forty, he fell into a deep depression and decided that he was getting old. He rejected any interest women showed in him. He would either criticize them for "just being nice" or he would wonder what was wrong with them (a projection of his own perfectionism) that they could be interested in a relationship with him.

Procrastination is as endless and futile as perfectionism. As long as we try to be perfect before entering the mainstream of life, we can be assured that our loneliness will continue. Cal held tenaciously to the critical attitude of his parents and continued it throughout his life. He projected his obsession on others, insisting that, even with initial acceptance, they would soon see his "intolerable faults" and regret ever having become involved with him. He had consistently refused any kind of help, feeling it would be an acknowledgment of failure. In his late forties he began abusing drugs and alcohol. One morning he was found dead of an overdose of barbiturates and alcohol. It was never clear if his death was suicidal or accidental. In any case, Cal's obsession with perfection reached its ultimate manifestation: throughout his entire life he postponed living and finally literally criticized himself to death.

The Odd-Ball Syndrome

Chronically lonely people suffer a deep feeling of inadequacy, usually all their lives. Such feelings can convince any of us that there is something we lack or that we are too different and this is the cause of our loneliness. It is often bewildering that, despite our best efforts, we seem to be unable to sustain nourishing relationships and to discover how to create excitement and interest in our lives. Certainly the lonely try just as hard as anyone else (usually harder), yet somehow loneliness continues.

AS LONG AS WE CLING TO OUR OLD
EXPLANATIONS OF THE CAUSES OF OUR

LONELINESS, WE ARE NOT OPEN TO
NEW DISCOVERIES OF THE WAYS IN
WHICH WE SUSTAIN OUR LONELINESS
AND PREVENT OURSELVES FROM
BREAKING OUT OF IT.

A stalemate results when we conclude that we lack some quality or ability we imagine everybody else enjoys. We may be sincerely convinced forever that we are misfits. Then, not only do we believe that our negative self-image is unique, but our loneliness as well! Intellectually, of course, we realize that many other people are lonely. Yet we may remain convinced that our loneliness is abnormally intense.

Once we label ourselves "misfits," each new experience of rejection is apt to be seen as further evidence. We perpetuate a vicious cycle of growing anxiety and feelings of inadequacy which, in turn, enhance the likelihood of further rejection and more loneliness.

"People just don't like me. It's been that way all my life." This was Sylvia's comment during a weekend encounter group. "You'd think I had bad breath or something. I walk up to five or six people having a conversation and within minutes they all just melt away and I'm left standing alone. I'm friendly and outgoing. I like people. I'm reasonably attractive, have a good job and a good education. I meet a lot of people and often do develop friendships. But somehow they all end in short order. I have found this with both men and women. I just can't understand it. What am I? Some sort of odd-ball? What has everyone got that I haven't got?"

Sylvia was honestly perplexed about her loneliness and had long ago concluded that she was simply inferior. As the weekend continued, members of the group began expressing their irritation as she constantly interrupted them with a "helpful" thought she wanted to share. Others resented her barrage of questions and felt as if they were being interrogated. She was startled by these comments since no one had ever confronted her so honestly. Despite this new awareness and her best efforts, she found herself persisting. With each such incident and subsequent confrontation, she became more aware of her insensitivity and her shocking variety of mannerisms that irritated others. One group member put it aptly: "You're a takeover artist! When you join the discussion, there's no room for anyone else!"

It was a distressing weekend for Sylvia, yet it provided her with a direction she could work toward in her efforts to resolve her loneliness. She began to focus on developing her sensitivity, really listening and realizing the need of others to express themselves. She also began to break out of her intrusive "helpfulness." Much to her surprise, people now seemed more interesting to her. She began to see and hear them for the first time. As she later commented: "It's no longer puzzling why I have had such difficulty with people. My loneliness is no longer a mystery."

The "missing link," or other variations of the odd-ball syndrome, invariably turn out to be manifestations of longstanding avoidance of awareness about some obvious (to everyone else) and highly toxic attitudes or behavior patterns.

Yes, But . . .

When we complain to friends and family about our loneliness, we are usually offered advice. Well-meant attempts to provide answers are usually met with a "yes, but" explanation of why the suggestions won't work. The helpful person may continue, often over a period of years, to attempt to persuade us to try his or her suggestions. This kind of "sales promotion," usually undertaken out of love and concern, invariably proves futile.

A "yes, but" response reflects the rigid, negative attitude that dominates us when we have felt stuck in our loneliness over a prolonged period of time. It reflects a "closed system" attitude toward relations with ourselves and our world. Hence, such attempts just don't work.

When we are lonely, those who care about us often expend a great deal of energy trying to encourage us to try a new approach. Their "why don't you" attempts are either overly rejected or subtly sabotaged.

WHEN WE ARE LONELY, COMPLAINING
IS OFTEN A WAY OF MANIPULATING
PEOPLE INTO TRYING TO RESCUE US.

There is a gratification in the care and responsiveness which is often forthcoming. However, others are apt to become increasingly exhausted by these consistently spurned attempts and they may begin to avoid the lonely person even though they remain deeply concerned.

Most of us are reluctant to voice our irritation at listening to the constant complaints of those we care about. In such instances, subtle, often subconscious barriers gradually emerge and nourishing interaction diminishes. An example of this pattern is seen in relationships between two chronically lonely people who complain to each other about their misery. Such "friendships" often continue for years, even though each person may feel intense dislike and hostility toward the other. They choose to remain in the relationship rather than be even more isolated. Such interaction becomes increasingly poisonous and tends to exacerbate feelings that other people really don't care.

In other instances, when we are lonely we may become so argumentative that we wear out those who have persisted in trying to be helpful. As present relationships are exhausted by constant complaining and "yes, but" kinds of argument, we search endlessly for new people. When we cling to playing this kind of game, it is little wonder that we become increasingly cynical and begin to believe the world is filled with no one but uncaring people. We refuse to see that our "dumping" and disinterest in being nourishing ourselves inevitably pushes nourishing people away, leaving us with ever-increasing feelings of emptiness and futility.

Conclusion

Each of us sees the world in a unique manner based on personal experiences and highly subjective conclusions about reality. Within each of us is a dominant pattern of preconceived attitudes that largely determines how we experience our inner selves as well as others. While this is based on past learning, it is not, as some believe, an unalterable set of attitudes and behavior patterns. We can break out of loneliness when we become sufficiently frustrated and sufficiently aware of our own self-destructive attitudes and behavior which allow us to *continue* to create new loneliness.

> WHATEVER OUR INNER ATTITUDES
> TOWARD OURSELVES AND OUR
> WORLD, WE RADIATE THEM TO
> OTHERS, WHETHER WE KNOW IT OR
> NOT.

Self-nourishers radiate an attitude of self-love and self-appreciation that fosters mutually gratifying relationships. In contrast, chronically lonely people lack genuine feelings of intimacy with themselves. They are poor self-nourishers and consequently lack the ability to give the love that they are potentially capable of, even though they may not believe it.

When we become phobic about our loneliness, we create the very monster we most fear. We then believe that this product of our own fantasies may emerge and overwhelm us. This self-poisoning attitude comes to its inevitable fruition with the emergence of an overwhelming attitude of futility.

> WHEN WE ARE CONVINCED THAT WE
> CAN'T RESOLVE OUR LONELINESS, WE
> THEREBY ASSURE THE CONTINUED
> CREATION OF GREATER LONELINESS.

The sense of helplessness which we feel more and more strongly as a result of chronic loneliness is always our own distortion of reality. It is the blooming of the seeds of long-standing fears and anxieties. By means of our personal ingenuity we manage to convince ourselves that our loneliness is something more than a creation of our own psyche. In reality, this is all it ever is.

CHRONIC LONELINESS IS A STATE OF
MIND.

8

Lies About Loneliness

The myths that our society perpetuates about the causes of loneliness grossly distort this universal human reality and foster the belief that the resolution of loneliness is difficult and complex. These myths are overwhelmingly destructive since they reinforce the belief that circumstances are the cause of chronic loneliness. For example, many people are victimized by irrational guilt feelings and see loneliness as a punishment. Similarly, feelings of shame are often enhanced by the myth that loneliness reflects a failure to become the kind of person we should be. These myths in general reflect the "shoulds" and "should nots" of our culture. They poison us with false notions about loneliness which result in unreasonable expectations. We develop an inner attitude that makes our breaking out of loneliness seem far more complicated and laborious than it really is.

Loneliness Myth #1: Feelings of Loneliness Are Unnatural.

Like so many myths about emotional pain, this reinforces the attitude that unpleasant emotions are "bad" and that the pain of loneliness is an indication of personal inadequacy or abnormality. In our culture, emotional pain in general is considered a sign of weakness rather than a valuable inner message that a state of excessive deprivation exists.

THE PAIN OF LONELINESS IS THE
LANGUAGE OF THE BODY DEMANDING
THAT WE RESPOND TO OUR
EMOTIONAL NEEDS. IT IS A
STATEMENT FROM OUR BODY TELLING
US THAT OUR LIFE IS
UNSATISFACTORY.

Those who feel the pain of loneliness is unnatural usually consider it a reflection of their personal weakness. Victims of the myth that loneliness is unnatural believe that any kind of pain is best dealt with by avoidance or suppression.

Loneliness Myth #2: Loneliness Is Primarily Caused by Misfortunes, an Unhappy Childhood, or Other External Circumstances.

This myth reinforces the various "blaming games," in which we waste our energy finding excuses for our loneliness. It reinforces our belief and fear that our emotional growth has been stunted by past traumas or rejections that doom us to failure in any new attempts to relate in a more nourishing fashion. Belief in this myth lessens the possibility of becoming aware of our continuing creation of the loneliness.

All her life Marie heard her mother bemoan the "fact" that "Marie just doesn't know how to make friends." Marie grew up believing this myth. When she was seventeen, it took all her courage to attend monthly church dances. While she wanted very much to go, she was anxious that no one would ask her to dance or even talk to her, an experience she would find terribly humiliating.

On one occasion she arrived in a state of near panic. She immediately went to the restroom and remained there for fifteen minutes trying to calm herself. Mustering her courage, she returned to the dance, saw a girlfriend, and desperately began to converse with her. In a few minutes a man asked her girlfriend to dance, leaving Marie alone again. She noticed some people she knew slightly who were just sitting around talking. She thought of joining them but was afraid they might feel she was being intrusive. Instead, she walked over to the refreshment table for a glass of punch. She stood sipping her drink, trying to look relaxed, and growing more tense moment by moment. By the time she finished her drink, her courage ran out and she left. It had not been a half hour since she had arrived, and half of that time she had been in the restroom. The tension of being alone at a dance even for a few minutes was more than she could bear.

Her mother's rejection had convinced her that people didn't like her. It explained her belief that loneliness was inevitable for her. Actually Marie usually disappeared so quickly that the chances of her connecting with other people were minimal. Unless someone quickly approached her, she was gone! In addition to her fear of rejection, Marie felt that everyone else had long since learned how to relate to others. Since it was her pattern to leave quickly, people who knew her felt she was unfriendly and snobbish. Her friends often felt rejected when she left without a word. At dances it seemed to them that Marie would look around and, not seeing anyone interesting, decide not to waste her time and leave. They had no way of knowing what was really going on inside her. Marie, on the other hand, felt as if her anxiety and embarrassment were obvious to everyone.

Convinced that she was doomed to be rejected, she was completely blinded to a similar anxiety in her peers. She could not see *she* rejected others by ignoring and avoiding them. She did not realize how many people were interested in knowing her but perceived her inner anxiety as disinterest. In this way Marie sustained her loneliness.

Loneliness Myth #3: Loneliness Is a Sign of Failure.

We often feel ashamed or embarrassed when others are aware of our loneliness. Our culture has a taboo against being lonely that encourages us to try to conceal our loneliness. This, of course, denies any constructive resolution and places a double burden on our shoulders. All too often we not only bear the pain of our loneliness but must hide it as well! Such myths reinforce the idea that having needs is a confession of personal inadequacy or failure, which will put other people off. The myth implies that people who have needs are less appealing. There is some truth to this but only to the extent that if we do not face up to our needs and do the best we can to satisfy them, then we will feel emotionally deprived. And when we feel emotionally deprived, we have less to give.

Therefore, it is not hard to understand that when lonely people relate to each other, they often hide their needs and thereby abort a potential basis for a mutually nourishing relationship. Instead they believe that first they must become more adequate. More pain and anguish is the only outcome of our belief that we must "improve" before earning the right to respond to our needs and express them openly.

Loneliness Myth #4: Loneliness Is a Form of Punishment.

This myth easily victimizes us when we live dominated by feelings of guilt.

> AT LEAST NINETY-NINE PERCENT OF ALL THE GUILT EACH OF US FEELS IS IRRATIONAL.

Our vulnerability to irrational guilt may be manifested in feelings that we are bad and that loneliness is our punishment. The guilt-and-punishment myth is usually powerful enough to override our intellectual awareness of the irrational nature of our guilt. We continue to feel guilty anyhow.

Martha and Chet had been lovers in high school. After graduation Chet decided to get a job so that they could afford to marry immediately, but Martha felt this was a short-sighted attitude. She had always been determined to go to college so that she could later qualify for more interesting jobs at higher salaries. She suggested that they continue seeing each other and both go to college. Chet had always been interested in accounting, and his uncle, who owned a large accounting firm, had assured him of a promising future. But Chet didn't want to delay marriage any longer. He decided to work two or three years, accumulate some money, and go on to college after that. He went to work as a salesman, did very well, and asked Martha to live with him. Martha loved Chet and wanted very much to be with him, but she felt guilty about furthering her own education while he was postponing his so they could live together. However, Chet insisted, and Martha finally gave in.

College opened many new areas of interest to Martha. She explored various fields of study and began meeting a lot of new and interesting people. It was increasingly difficult to find friends whom they both enjoyed. Chet's friends were mostly salesmen whose wives were primarily preoccupied with their homes and children. He felt Martha's friends were too intellectual and lacked a down-to-earth quality.

During the next three years Martha became concerned about the growing difference in their interests and the increasing difficulty they had in finding things to share. She had been urging Chet to give up the apartment and start college. Chet agreed but kept postponing it, and a year later Martha graduated with a bachelor's degree.

The crisis in their relationship came when Martha announced that she had been accepted to law school out of state. Chet was furious. He felt he had been betrayed. He accused Martha of having used him to get her education. She insisted she had always made it clear that it was her intent to become a professional. She also reminded him how he had continuously postponed his own education.

In the weeks that followed they fought and argued. Chet asked Martha to apply to a local law school so that they could be together. She refused. One night after both had been drinking they had a particularly violent argument that ended when Chet ran out of the house, got in his car, and sped away. Three hours later the phone rang. Chet had crashed his car into a wall and was in the hospital. He had broken his back and would be laid up for months.

Martha felt very guilty about Chet's accident. She tried to assure herself that it was not her fault, that she had the right to make her own decision about her life, and that Chet's getting drunk and speeding away in his car was his responsibility. Nevertheless, the guilt gnawed at her. She spent all the time she could with Chet. He was still bedridden when she left for law school. At their final meeting Chet's last words to her were: "I never want to see you again and may God forgive you for what you've done to me."

Chet's statement haunted Martha for years. She sought to lose herself in her studies and graduated with honors. She was immediately hired by a top law firm and did exceedingly well. She was a dedicated professional and was also aware that she was, out of guilt, continuing to use her work as a way to avoid any new involvement with men. When she occasionally accepted a date, she found herself thinking of Chet and feeling a sinking sensation in her stomach. Despite her efforts to reassure herself that her guilt feelings were unreasonable, they persisted and she again stopped dating.

In her middle thirties she felt an increasing loneliness that she was unable to escape even with her busy professional life. Her loneliness had become the symbol of her guilt and subsequently her self-inflicted punishment for leaving Chet.

Loneliness Myth #5: Introverts Are Lonelier than Extroverts.

A common misconception is that those who are outgoing and surround themselves with people are less lonely. This myth ignores the games lonely people play in order to distract themselves from their loneliness or to hide it from others. Extroverts who are chronically lonely may sustain this facade over a lifetime. In contrast, so this myth goes, the introvert, who spends more time in solitude or has less contact with people, is assumed to be more susceptible to loneliness.

Introversion and extroversion are matters of degree rather than completely distinct personality categories. One's general orientation may suggest the most appropriate resolutions to loneliness. However, such variations in personality patterns per se have little or nothing to do with the loneliness.

Loneliness Myth #6: Women Are More Often Lonely than Men.

This popular notion reflects many myths about the differences between the sexes. In men, loneliness derogates masculinity. Boys are taught that "real men" do not give in to their emotional pain, least of all show it to others. Thus, men tend to hide their loneliness more frequently than do women. Our culture is more accepting of emotional expression in women, although this too is apt to be misconstrued as an indication of the "weaker sex." Compared to men, women are simply less inhibited about openly acknowledging their loneliness.

Loneliness Myth #7: Sexually Attractive People Are Less Lonely.

The strong cultural value we place on physical attractiveness makes it appear a guarantee against loneliness. Those who are lonely and do not feel they are attractive often believe that loneliness is rarely a problem for people with a lot of sex appeal. This "if only I were sexier" defense against loneliness easily becomes an endless detour in which enormous effort is continually devoted to physical appearance. While attractive people may enjoy more approaches from others, the resolution of loneliness through nourishing relationships is not found in the ability to attract people. Relationships based only on physical attraction are characteristically of short duration. In building and sustaining deeper intimacy, sexual attractiveness assumes a diminishing role when the relationship continues over a long time. People seldom give first priority to physical attractiveness in seeking enduring one-to-one relationships. For example, most of us would not state that we chose our spouse primarily because he or she was the most sexually exciting person available. Those of us who have discovered through our own experiences that sex itself cannot sustain a relationship usually resolve loneliness.

Wilma was thirty-six when her husband suddenly announced he had met someone else and wanted a divorce. While the suddenness was quite a shock, it was actually no surprise. For several years, she had felt that they were drifting away from each other. Dennis was a building contractor and had gradually developed a pattern of working longer hours and going out of town on business trips more frequently. For her part, Wilma had been busy raising their two children, maintaining their home, and pursuing various interests. She had long ago stopped initiating sex and, on those infrequent occasions when Dennis approached her, she accommodated him dutifully.

After Dennis left, Wilma began trying to understand how they had drifted away from each other initially. During the ten years of their marriage she had gained considerable weight and had gradually become less interested in her appearance. She concluded that the marriage had broken up because she had lost interest in looking sexy.

She went on a diet, bought more attractive clothes, and generally began taking better care of herself. She had plastic surgery on her face and breasts. It seemed at first that her program was working. She began dating extensively and over the next several years had a number of affairs. However, none of these lasted more than a few months. She became aware of a pattern in which each relationship began with an intense physical attraction which gradually waned and ended.

She persisted in remaining preoccupied with her physical attractiveness, giving little thought to developing her own interests and needs, other than through relationships with men. She ignored comments men would make about her critical nature, her demands and expectations of how a "real" man should act.

She was forty when she panicked about being alone the rest of her life. Out of desperation she reluctantly decided to go into therapy. She became aware of her anxiety that being open and giving would make her unbearably vulnerable to rejection. With this and other insights, she began to see the basis of her loneliness. Gradually she broke out of her expectations about how people, especially men, should be and how they should relate to her. Even more important in resolving her loneliness, she grew to respect herself and, subsequently, became more giving and accepting of others. The quality of her relationships with men deepened, and, for the first time in her life, she began appreciating deep friendships with other women. She saw that her relationships with men had been so overwhelmingly sexual that, as the initial passion of each romance diminished, there was little else to broaden the relationship and give it substance.

Many people of both sexes follow a pattern that amounts to an endless series of one-to-one relationships lasting from a few months to a year or so. The dating game begins again until a new and similar relationship is found. This cycle, once started, recurs consistently. Often it is a reflection of the myth that sexual attraction is the key to intimacy.

For most of us, physical attraction is an essential aspect of our one-to-one relationships, but it is not enough to sustain growing intimacy.

As Wilma became aware of this, her relations with men changed. She was fifty when she chose between two prospective husbands. Her second marriage was healthy and intimate. Her feelings for her husband grew and deepened as the years went by. In addition, and much to her surprise, she found that she and her husband both enjoyed sex more than ever.

A deepening intimacy based on mutual trust and love is the basis of an enduring relationship which is subsequently reflected in deeply satisfying sex. Many people have the cart and the horse reversed.

Loneliness Myth #8: Growing Old Makes Loneliness Almost Inevitable.

Although we may believe that maturity will resolve our childhood loneliness, chronically lonely people feel that the likelihood of resolving their loneliness lessens as they grow older. Women often fear that the likelihood of lasting intimate relationships begins to lessen drastically after the age of thirty. With men, forty is the age associated with the fear of growing older and lonely. Both sexes fear loneliness in middle age, particularly when a fulfilling life-style has not been established. Fears of loneliness in both sexes begin to increase beyond the middle years.

Ages fifty and sixty-five are perceived as significant milestones. At these ages, popular myth teaches us, loneliness and aging are practically synonymous, and it is futile to continue seeking intimacy or a new, more creative life-style.

Fifty-five-year-old Carl had been married and divorced twice. He was a warm, fun-loving person who enjoyed people. He could accept those qualities in each person that he didn't particularly care for without feeling critical or disappointed. A wealthy, attractive man, he dated women of all ages.

He said frankly that: "Young women really turn me on." But he was also aware that, because of their differences in values, interests, and experiences, these relationships soon became boring, aside from sex. Most of his men friends of about his age were more interested in dating younger women and would almost automatically reject women over forty. However, for Carl, many of these women were sexually attractive and, in addition, had greater emotional maturity, awareness, and sensitivity. As he kiddingly put it: "My problem is that I find so many interesting women and so little competition from other men that it is difficult for me to make up my mind!"

For Carl, age meant little since his own self-esteem and the enjoyment and interest he felt about life were so profound. Sharing this with someone of like mind was far more important to him than physical attractiveness. Carl summarized his attitude: "When I was younger I was really macho. I mainly wanted to impress women with what a good lover I was. I used to delight in other men envying the attractive women I dated. Now I want a deeper kind of relationship with a woman. I call it 'soul-to-soul contact.' When I feel this kind of rapport my sexual interest heightens and my enjoyment of sex has a depth of fulfillment that I never knew existed when I was younger."

Older people who are lonely and believe that their age is responsible deny themselves in various ways. They may limit their relationships by categorizing people by age and then consuming themselves with their destructive beliefs in the myths associated with each age group. For example, women who are attracted to men years younger than themselves often suppress their feelings because of the myth that the man should at least be their age or older. Men, in turn, often prefer women older than themselves.

This myth also reinforces the negative notion that age brings an immutable quality to attitudes and behavior patterns. It is often assumed that older people have lost the ability to compromise in developing new relationships. To the degree that they believe this myth, they enhance the likelihood of remaining lonely.

The myth relating loneliness to aging is largely a reflection of our cultural attitude toward older people. It is more socially acceptable to complain about loneliness as we grow older, but feeling that age per se is responsible for loneliness is a myth.

OUR ATTITUDE ABOUT AGING CREATES
OUR LONELINESS.

Loneliness Myth #9: Our Loneliness Will End When We Find the "Right Person."

This myth is a reflection of the pervasive romantic fantasy exemplified in the typical Hollywood "boy-meets-girl" movies of the 1930s and 40s, in which the hero and/or heroine find true love and live happily ever after. While we may know it is romantic escapism, we may still adopt this kind of passive, helpless attitude and hope that one person will be the answer. People often are trapped by their insistence that loving someone will end their loneliness.

Loneliness Myth #10: If Others Were More Loving and Giving Toward Us We Would Not Be Lonely.

The lonelier we become, the more we tend to feel paranoid. This myth in particular is a manifestation of the paranoia that is prevalent when we feel intense loneliness. We become increasingly defensive and distrustful of others and we cling to our suspicions while we wait for others to convince us that they really care. We stack the deck against ourselves, as the evidence of the sincerity of others is seldom sufficient to reassure us. In reality, there is no guaranteed security in any relationship despite the best of intentions. One way to assure ourselves of continued loneliness is to put the responsibility on others to convince us that they really care and will continue to do so.

Loneliness Myth #11: The Way to Resolve Loneliness Is to Develop More Interests and Activities.

Like so many myths about loneliness, this one is based on the false notion that the resolution of loneliness is to be found "out there," rather than within ourselves. For example, if we were better educated, or more informed, or more interesting, we could more easily find intimacy and resolve our loneliness. All myths contain some truth. However, when we are lonely, we distort this partial truth to convince ourselves that, if we were always stimulating or had interesting information to share, we could sustain an intimate relationship. This belief is a form of avoidance, in which the major effort in relating to others is an attempt to become a walking encyclopedia of knowledge and current events to keep conversation going. This kind of dialogue more readily leads to boredom than to intimacy.

Loneliness Myth #12: Wealthy, Successful, or Socially Prominent People Are Less Lonely than Others.

Like the preceding myth, this one ignores the quality in each person's life. Many "successful" people, out of fear of vulnerability, impose a self-limiting attitude on the depth and intensity of their relations with others. Their relating is often limited to a specific purpose, in order to accomplish certain goals: for example, the business person who is largely interested in relating to people who are potential customers. Success, and the social recognition that usually comes with it, offer a ready-made facade behind which lonely people can hide. Frequently they are not really aware of how lonely (emotionally deprived) they are, since their feelings of loneliness are often masked by other factors such as the pressure and stress of busy schedules, fatigue, medical problems, or the habitual use of drugs, tranquilizers, or alcohol.

Loneliness Myth #13: Chronic Loneliness Is Irreversible.

Intense feelings of loneliness are, for many people, a lifelong experience. This makes it difficult to believe that we can break out of the state of loneliness we have always known.

Consequently, we tend to create a self-perpetuating despair about ever resolving our loneliness. The conviction that we are stuck increases as we grow older and continue to feel deeply lonely. Each new episode of intense loneliness is interpreted as validation of the fear that it is too late.

Loneliness Myth #14: Breaking Out of Loneliness Is a Complicated Process.

This myth suggests that there is something profound that must be understood before we can even hope to see a resolution to our loneliness. For example, when we allow this myth to dominate our thoughts, we may believe that we will remain lonely until our past guilts, failings, and resentments have been dealt with.

Breaking out of loneliness calls for direct confrontation with ourselves in order to gain awareness of how our attitudes and behavior perpetuate our loneliness. In contrast, unraveling all the events and traumas of the past only postpones coping with loneliness. Focusing on the past can be an endless process since there is always new material to be dealt with. Living in the present means experiencing each moment. This is where we find real emotional nourishment and the resolution to loneliness.

9

~~~~~~~~~~

Find What You're Really
Afraid Of

"Paranoia" is a descriptive term which includes the tendency to project to others our own thoughts, feelings, and fears. In this sense, all of us are paranoid to one degree or another, for none of us is completely objective. In fact, total objectivity is not a human quality. All we can say is that usually we are sufficiently in touch with reality to function reasonably well.

Loneliness intensifies our paranoia and, as our paranoia increases, the threats and rejections we imagine are emanating toward us from the external world also intensify. When we continue to feel lonely we are trapped in an increasingly dangerous cycle in which loneliness and paranoia mutually reinforce each other. This, in turn, leads to tremendous anxiety and a growing reluctance to confront these fantasies. We become phobic about the risk of expressing our fear of rejection to see whether others are indeed feeling rejecting toward us or whether our fear is totally self-induced.

When feeling paranoid, our attention is focused primarily on the outside world instead of on ourselves. Thus, our inner potential, which could be utilized to resolve our loneliness, is relegated to a secondary position. What others think is more important than what *we* think.

Various patterns of loneliness emerge as a consequence of this self-induced helplessness.

PARANOIA CREATES A CHRONIC
STATE OF IMPOTENCY AND FEAR.

We await (with fear and anger) the fate that these fearful external forces, through our own projections, will decree.

THE MORE PARANOID WE FEEL, THE
MORE REJECTING WE FEEL TOWARD
OTHERS. THIS IS EXTERNALIZED (IT'S
NOT ME—IT'S THEM) AND WE THEN
FEEL REJECTED.

This pattern is a major factor in the impotent feeling characteristic of the chronically lonely. When we feel impotent we can be certain of a growing resentment within us, whether we are aware of it or not. This culminates in an anger–fear pattern that is mutually reinforcing: fear generates anger, which in turn generates more fear. It is then natural to relate overtly to the world, with the focal point being on our fear. The next downward step is to hide and isolate ourselves by means of various facades, games, and manipulations of the self, all of which are intended to give the appearance of "nice guys." Or, when our anger is overt, we attack through criticisms and complaints and, in general, taking the role of judge. Others are rejecting us, and that's why we are angry.

When we feel paranoid, we openly or secretly criticize our friends, family, even acquaintances. Usually, everyone is found lacking in some way.

AS LONG AS WE CLING TO OUR
PARANOIA, WE CAN'T SATISFY OR
ACCEPT OURSELVES OR FEEL
ACCEPTING TOWARD OTHERS; HENCE,
OUR CONTINUED LONELINESS IS
ASSURED.

It is safe to assume that when we are lonely, we will continue to externalize our frustrations. We are likely to continue complaining, which is a not-so-subtle manifestation of the anger and hostility associated with paranoia. We remain stalemated in angry helplessness and avoid taking the responsibility for resolving our loneliness.

Since rejection is both a constant and unavoidable aspect of living (every time anyone says "no" it *is* a rejection), there are always events that we can use to build a case that people don't like us and that our fears are not imaginary. The last deadly step in the paranoid process occurs when we generalize about the rejections in our day-to-day living and conclude that reaching out and continuing to take risks is foolish and will only lead to more pain and rejection. A sense of isolation grows as we build more walls to protect against any vulnerability. Our world becomes increasingly restricted and isolated, while our growing feelings of alienation and loneliness enhances our anger. This leads to the vicious cycle of fear, concealment, and projection of the angry paranoia of our loneliness. Relationships are dominated by suspicion and hostility. People are seen as "them," and our isolation and continued loneliness become fixated.

I Hurt So Easily

Paranoia, especially when we feel lonely, makes us see ourselves as emotionally delicate. The fear of rejection can become so powerful and anxiety-producing that we convince ourselves that rejection would indeed be unbearable. The slightest hint of rejection can trigger catastrophic expectations, and a relationship is over before it can become intimate. The principal tactic in paranoia is to reject *first*, thereby avoiding the possibility of being rejected. This feeling of emotional delicacy creates an endless cycle of distrust, withdrawal, and the erection of new, more imposing barriers.

However, such defenses never provide any satisfying feeling of security. The growing deprivation of needed contact is also intensified with increasing emotional isolation. A toxic cycle is generated in which new defenses are offset by the intensifying pressure of growing loneliness, leading to more defenses. This process is endless since, in each of us, the need for human contact continues to press relentlessly.

LIVING IN FANTASY GENERALLY
MAKES US MORE EMOTIONALLY
DELICATE SINCE WE AVOID LEARNING
THROUGH ACTUAL EXPERIENCES HOW
TO COPE WITH EMOTIONAL PAIN.

Experiencing rejection is essential in learning to tolerate the emotional pain that accompanies it. It is extremely rare that our experience is as devastating and endlessly painful as we fantasize. But we can only discover this through our own experience.

There is no way to avoid the endless stalemate that results from the destructive cycle of paranoia and loneliness except to become aware of our continuous self-entrapment. However, when the pain is sufficiently intense and we are aware of the emotional expense of our paranoia, we develop a powerful motivation to take a new look at our self-induced loneliness. Then the willingness to take risks may gradually emerge.

Each of us must learn for ourselves, in our own time, in our own way, how to reach out and take emotional risks. Similarly, each of us can only discover through experiencing our own emotional pain that we can tolerate it, recover, and continue on. When we feel chronically lonely, this is a vital aspect in sustaining our determination to persist in seeking the most suitable pathways to the resolution of loneliness. The alternative is to remain locked in paranoia and to continue living on the sidelines of life, feeling deprived, angry, and frustrated.

Loneliness Is My Secret

A hallmark of chronic loneliness is an air of secrecy about being lonely. It is another manifestation of the domination of paranoia. When we are lost in paranoia, we usually consider any admission of loneliness tantamount to inviting more rejection. Similarly, we may avoid confronting ourselves with our loneliness. In a sense, we play hide-and-go-seek with ourselves.

VULNERABILITY IS THE LAST THING
THE PARANOID PERSON IS WILLING TO
SHOW TO OTHERS OR TO FACE
INWARDLY.

When we are dominated by our paranoia, it feels safer to see the world as a hostile conspiracy. This is a projection of our own alienation from ourselves. Vulnerability is seen as a form of foolishness, while secrecy is seen as the most prudent way of surviving.

It is not surprising, then, that lonely people are themselves extremely hostile, although this emotion is usually hidden by a mask of superficial friendliness. This is a manifestation of the affinity between loneliness and paranoia. We fail to see that our closed-in, rigid attitude is *our* rejection of others; instead we project this onto the world and see ourselves as innocent victims.

> THE PARANOIA OF LONELINESS CAN
> BECOME A WAY OF LIFE IN WHICH
> THE CHRONICALLY LONELY PERSON
> FOREVER AVOIDS LIVING IN THE
> REALITY OF THE PRESENT.

We have lost our senses when we allow ourselves to fall victim to the paranoia of loneliness. We do not see or hear or experience what is actually occurring around us. The distortions from our own projections dominate our perception. We do a deaf, dumb, and blind act, in which our reactions are rigidly based on expectations of rejection. We distort any data from our ongoing experiences that do not fit into these preconceived expectations. Ironic as it may seem, genuine love and nourishment are met with distrust or ignored entirely.

> PARANOIA IS THE ROYAL ROAD TO
> CHRONIC LONELINESS.

While the paranoia that may dominate our behavior when we feel deeply lonely is our own fantasy, we believe that we see the world accurately. We are convinced that being open and trusting is responsible for many of our past hurts. Clinging to the past is precisely how we lose touch with ourselves. These attitudes originated in relationships with people who are either no longer important in our lives or need not be. Yet we are convinced that, should we again become open and vulnerable, we will only be hurt again.

In the lives of chronically lonely people, the trauma of past rejections by one or a handful of people fosters the fear that distorts how they relate to people.

THE PARANOID PERSON
AUTOMATICALLY AND IMMEDIATELY
PROJECTS ONTO EACH NEW PERSON
ALL KINDS OF THREATENING
ATTRIBUTES FROM THE PAST.

The most crucial past relationships usually occurred during childhood with parents or parental figures. In adulthood, when traumas between the now-grown child and his or her parents are reviewed, there is usually only the slightest agreement, if any, about what actually happened. This is a classic example of projecting. Each person is convinced her or his particular perception of what happened is correct and the other person just won't admit it!

Another distortion of reality in such instances is a perception of oneself as just as helpless and powerless as when these feelings initially developed in childhood. This fantasy prevents lonely people from learning how to relate to others in a more nourishing way, as well as how to protect themselves more realistically and, therefore, more effectively. It is ironic that the chronically lonely, who so desperately need to open themselves to new learning, are the last to use their ongoing experiences to become gradually more effective both in relating to others and in coping with rejection. Instead, they persist in using new experiences to reinforce their chronic paranoid pattern by focusing only on the similarities between present experiences and those based on obsolete and painful relationships from the past.

When we feel lonely and are caught up in our paranoia, we expect to be abused and manipulated. Any honest approach is met with suffocating suspicion and distrust: "Why should he or she want to know me? What are they after?"

Such paranoid statements create psychological barriers against even ordinary, casual contact. We continue literally to drive others away. Despite intense emotional deprivation and deep longing for intimacy, our paranoia actually precipitates our rejection of others.

> THE REFUSAL TO MEET ANOTHER
> PERSON HALFWAY (AND USUALLY
> EVEN ONE FOURTH OF THE WAY) IS
> PARANOID.

When we remain blinded by our paranoia, we fail to see that the guardedness, suspicion, and intensity with which we protect ourselves is the way in which we make others feel rejected.

Candy was strikingly beautiful, the twenty-two-year-old daughter of an equally beautiful mother. When the two of them were together, they could easily pass for sisters. Candy's mother had a long-standing paranoid hostility toward men and she had closed herself off from them. She had a number of affairs beginning when she was fifteen and culminating in Candy's illegitimate birth. Candy's father had insisted on an abortion, and when Candy's mother refused, he left and was never heard from again. From that time on, her paranoia deepened.

Her mother methodically indoctrinated Candy with the idea that "men only want one thing." In high school, Candy was known as a tease. She was unusually attractive and flirtatious, yet allowed no sexual intimacy. Her flirting was simply a way of "proving" what her mother had taught her.

Several men had been in love with her, made no sexual demands, and wanted a relationship on any basis. Her mother encouraged her to take what she could get from them while reminding her of what each man ultimately had in mind.

Candy accepted a marriage proposal from an extremely wealthy man, whom she had become very fond of. Still playing her mother's game of vengeance, she kept postponing the date, implying that she wasn't sure he really loved her. She insisted that she was determined to remain a virgin until they were married. This, she found, was the easiest way to avoid his sexual approaches.

Her fiancé accepted her chastity, as he was totally devoted to her. After three years, he told her that although he loved her deeply, he felt it best they end their engagement. Candy agreed to set a date and subsequently reneged as before. This time her fiancé broke their engagement and she was outraged. Yet when he suggested they marry immediately, she again refused. When he left, she was angry and bitter. Her mother's response was that this was more proof that "you just can't trust men." Only when he left did Candy realize how much she loved him. Now that he was no longer a threat, she could drop her paranoid distrust and allow her feelings to emerge.

Why Me?

Paranoia can be seen as an attitude that teaches us to believe that we are victims of circumstances, the cruelty of others, and all kinds of undeserved abuses. "Why me?" is a common cry of lonely victims of their own paranoia as they struggle against a world they see united in its rejection.

> BECAUSE OF THEIR PARANOIA, LONELY PEOPLE ARE UNABLE TO TAKE RESPONSIBILITY FOR THEIR LONELINESS. THE NOTION THAT THEY CAUSE THEIR OWN LONELINESS SEEMS ABSURD.

When we are unable to accept the idea that others see the world differently, we fail to gain a true understanding of our relationships. Instead we project our own narrow concepts onto others and thereby invalidate the individuality of those who seek to relate to us. Our perception of others is narrowed by our own limited viewpoint, so that we lack empathy with other people whose perception is equally valid, though different. The refusal to consider the possibility that others are as sincere (and frightened) as we are is the basic attitude with which we actively reject others, although most of us would deny that we do this. Knowingly or not, we ourselves sustain our emotional deprivation and paranoid alienation. As long as we cling to the pseudo-safety of our paranoia, our continued loneliness is assured.

10

༄

How to Stop Being Afraid to Love

Since sexuality usually plays a major role in our lives, most of us have enormous expectations about what it is supposed to do for our intimate relationships. Our attitudes about sex can reinforce self-induced loneliness when they mislead us in understanding the real significance of intimacy. For example, our society's acceptance of sexual freedom encourages us to escape into sex to avoid loneliness. Usually there is at least a temporary easing of our loneliness when we are involved in an intense sexual relationship; however, relationships based primarily on sexual attraction may be totally lacking in real intimacy. There may be little of the caring and emotional sharing necessary to resolve the deeper feelings of deprivation so prevalent when we feel lonely.

No one who knew him would have believed that Nick was a chronically lonely man. He was filled with shame and embarrassment at the thought of anyone knowing how lonely he was. Women found him quite attractive and he knew it. He had an active sex life, but seemed to lose interest quickly in each affair. His relationships with women were almost entirely limited to sex. On more than one occasion he met a woman he had had a brief affair with and did not even remember her name. Nick had an intense fear of being alone, especially at night, and women were his way of avoiding this. He always maintained relationships with several women who were available on short notice. They had no inkling of his intense loneliness. He knew these relationships were not really satisfying, yet he continued this pattern of moving on from one woman to the next.

In his late forties, the intensity of his loneliness had heightened. Over the years his way of using his sexual attractiveness had become less effective, and the relief from loneliness it had provided was increasingly unsatisfying.

Nick's pattern exemplifies how each of us, when we are lonely, may choose to use particular assets or strong points to avoid facing our loneliness. His active sex life, plus the use of alcohol, enabled him to avoid the real issue: his fear of intimacy. Sex made his life tolerable and at times pleasurable.

People who are sexually promiscuous are not necessarily lonely. This may simply be their preference. However, when we are chronically lonely, a preoccupation with sexual gratification at least suggests the possibility that we may be using sex to avoid deeper, more threatening fears. In such instances, sex ultimately becomes a way of creating loneliness.

> BECAUSE OF THE INTENSITY OF THE
> EMOTIONAL EXPERIENCE, IT IS EASY
> TO MISTAKE SEXUAL INTIMACY FOR
> MORE MEANINGFUL AND LOVING
> EMOTIONAL INVOLVEMENT.

Some of the women in Nick's life had their own pattern of self-induced loneliness which complemented his. They would cling to their hope for a more intimate relationship with him in spite of the fact that he gave no indication that this would ever happen. Nick always shrugged off any comments to this effect with glib phrases about not wanting to settle down. There were two women who had been in love with Nick for years and refused to face up to the futility and unhappiness they felt by settling for infrequent encounters, which only intensified their loneliness and lack of fulfillment. They knew sex per se was not enough, yet they remained unwilling to let go of him.

Any source of nourishment can be misused. Sexuality can lead to a deepening intimacy, or it can destroy the development of intimacy. This occurs frequently in lonely people who distort their sexuality by falling victim to what they believe is the normal, "hip" way of relating sexually. Many lonely people create their loneliness by taking sex lightly, knowing all the while that they are being dishonest with themselves.

> MORE EMOTIONAL PAIN AND DISTRESS
> ARE LIKELY WHEN WE BELIEVE THAT
> SEX IS AN EFFECTIVE WAY OF
> RESOLVING OUR LONELINESS.

It is a myth that being sufficiently attractive sexually and "good in bed" will lead to intimacy. While sex is usually an essential part of an intimate adult relationship, it cannot, in and of itself, provide the emotional nourishment which fosters enduring intimacy. For most of us, particularly when we have been lonely for some time, this is difficult to accept. For those who see themselves as sexually unattractive, the myth that sex and intimacy are the same readily becomes an excuse for their loneliness (if I were more attractive, I wouldn't be lonely). This limited attitude about the sexual aspect of relationships narrows the lonely person's perspective of the full meaning of intimate relating.

The typical self-induced pattern of loneliness in such instances involves a series of love affairs. Mutual feelings of love are felt and expressed, yet somehow these involvements always seem to dissipate despite a good sexual relationship. Unless there is a firmer basis on which to develop more lasting intimacy, sexual excitement gradually wanes, and with it the relationship.

> HOWEVER GRATIFYING OUR SEX LIFE
> MAY BE, IT IS NOT SUFFICIENT IN
> ITSELF TO SUSTAIN AN INTIMATE
> RELATIONSHIP OR TO RESOLVE OUR
> LONELINESS.

Some lonely people believe they can resolve their problem by being great sex partners. They are willing to give up their own gratification to focus on satisfying their partner, in the hope that he or she will want to continue the relationship. This in turn (so the game goes) will resolve their loneliness. Any lack of satisfaction is ignored or at most quietly resented. For example, a man may hurry the sex act, insisting that this is simply a manifestation of his intense passion. In such instances, the woman who plays this game may fear that expressing her wish that he slow down will break the illusion that they are sexually compatible. Or she may fake orgasm to build up his ego and sustain the illusion that they have a mutually gratifying relationship. In this way, she may hope she will be able to "hold" the man, deepen their relationship, and end her loneliness.

While sex can enhance the quality of a relationship and lead to deeper intimacy, this is not an automatic sequence.

SEX HAS NO INTRINSIC QUALITY OF INTIMACY.

Traditionally, most men can enjoy sex with a woman without even knowing her name. They are simply attracted to her body. With changing attitudes, women, too, are more able to experience similar pleasure. But sex for sex's sake, while mutually delightful, cannot alleviate loneliness.

Many lonely people have their egos so strongly involved in their sexual performance that sex becomes an ego trip. This is particularly true, for example, in those who seek to control others sexually and who delude themselves into believing that being sexually desired will resolve their loneliness.

Another frequent pattern is an obsessive attitude about sex, in which quantity is seen as a substitute for intimacy. The basic premise is that by waking up in bed with a different person every morning feelings of loneliness will be dispelled. But the next morning often tells the story clearly. Either one or both may awaken with an intense need to get away from the other now that their sexual appetites have been satisfied. Such experiences only intensify feelings of loneliness and rejection.

Thunder-and-Lightning Relationships

A new romance usually begins with great sexual excitement. Such thunder-and-lightning relationships may be the beginning of lasting intimacy. However, when we are lonely we tend to jump to the conclusion that "this is it." In so doing we are apt to avoid facing what would otherwise be clearly evident, i.e., that various aspects of the other person warn of important incompatibilities. When we use sex to alleviate our loneliness we are apt to live in a cyclical pattern of peaks of elation and joy when we are romantically involved, followed by black despair when the relationship ends and there is more loneliness. While it is common for a couple to argue and afterwards enjoy unusually satisfying lovemaking, it is another matter when sex is used to compensate for the lack of a more broadly based compatibility that includes the many other dimensions of intimate living.

When we are lonely, our discrimination tends to lessen, and we are more apt to become involved in a sexual relationship with others whose attitudes, beliefs, and values are irreconcilable with our own, knowing full well that these differences cannot be avoided indefinitely.

Sooner or later, basic incompatibilities in any relationship will emerge, sex becomes less and less effective in sustaining intimacy, and eventually the relationship ends.

Sexual Freedom and Loneliness

Those whose relationships are primarily sexual tend to follow a pattern of continuously changing sex partners. Such relationships lack stability since the avoidance of any extensive commitment is essential. It is our responsibility, when we choose sexual freedom, to be aware that such relationships are likely to remain transitory and superficial and cannot provide a feeling of belonging. Multiple relationships move us in an opposite direction from deeper, more enduring, intimate relationships. Those who choose to enjoy sexual contact with any number of people are simply adopting a different attitude from those who consider sex as one aspect of a total, more intimate relationship. Either choice has its consequences; rarely, if ever, can we choose one thing without giving up something else.

When we wish to resolve our loneliness, it is important to realize that there is a deeper meaning to sexuality in a relationship of exclusive commitment. Otherwise we may deceive ourselves into believing that passion and the temporary relief it brings from the pain of our loneliness is acceptable for the present and that later on we will settle down and seek deeper, fuller, intimate relationships.

MARGARET:

For years I worried about turning thirty. I told myself it was a state of mind I could ignore. My friends gave me a birthday party and I got a lot of ribbing about being over the hill. That night, after the party, I felt a deep sense of despair! I suddenly felt I was getting old!

From the time I left college I had many periods of loneliness which I attributed to not being married or involved with someone. Whenever I was going with someone my loneliness would subside. I would work hard at building the relationship, hoping it would lead to marriage. I tried everything to keep a man interested. I thought that sex was the key. I felt unbelievably intense anxiety about pleasing a man sexually. My sexual needs became less important as I focused on what he wanted. I hoped he would eventually grow to care for me as a person. There have been four men I've been deeply in love with. Within a year, each of these relationships either ended or dwindled down to occasional dating.

My friends kept telling me that I should play hard to get, but I felt this was dishonest. When I was going with a man I was interested in, he could call me anytime and I would change my plans to be with him. Each of my relationships followed the same pattern. At first, we would see each other several times a week and spend the night together. We would go out for dinner and dancing or we would go away for the weekend. Gradually we spent more and more time at either his apartment or mine. We stopped going out to dinner and, instead, I cooked. I kept quiet for fear of appearing demanding. The pattern settled into a Saturday night dinner, usually at my apartment, after which we made love and went to sleep. He left early in the morning with some excuse. Still I said nothing. At times I got angry with myself for being so accommodating and dishonest. Still, it seemed to be the best I could do.

I'm afraid I'll appear demanding, as my mother was toward my father. I'm even more fearful that men will think I'm a bitch if I get angry. Sex is now a dull routine for me. I feel like nothing more than an object to satisfy the man's sexual needs. What really makes me angry is that putting up with all this doesn't seem to help in the least. If I say "no" to a man, I never hear from him again. I still don't understand why I never seem to find the deeper, more intimate relationship I've always wanted.

Margaret is clinging to her belief that being sexually available and exciting leads to deeper intimacy. Despite her good intentions, she ignores her own needs, shares very little of her deeper self, and knows even less about her lovers.

In therapy, she began to realize that these relationships were actually quite boring to her. She remembered how conversations dwindled into nothing more than idle chatter, listening to music, or watching television.

Subsequently, as Margaret herself became more open she broke out of her games and related to men more honestly. Breaking out of her conviction that sex would keep a man interested was a painful process. Indeed, some men whom she liked but didn't want to have sex with immediately did not call again. However, she now realized the folly of giving in sexually in the hope that her capitulation would lead to the kind of intimacy she wanted.

She was thirty-four when she met Dan. He had been divorced for three years. By now she was at ease, being open and honest. Dan also was tired of what he called "sex games." As they increasingly shared their inner selves with each other, their love deepened, and she enjoyed the most satisfying relationship of her life.

A year later Margaret and Dan married. Their marriage flourished and became a source of a fuller life than she had ever dreamed possible. She continued to be surprised that the more she focused on her own growth, the more attractive she seemed to Dan.

> WHEN WE ARE LONELY, WE OFTEN
> SUSTAIN LONELINESS BY CONSISTENTLY
> RELATING SEXUALLY TO PEOPLE WE
> KNOW ARE NOT INTERESTED IN
> FULLER RELATIONSHIPS.

11

❧❧❧❧❧❧

The Secret Loneliness of Marriage

VICKI:

Lately I've really been feeling left out. My friends are either going with someone or are married. I'm not a couple with anybody. I find myself alone . . . and that really bothers me. I feel very lonely. I feel distant even from my best girlfriends. They're all with a guy and they have good, involved relationships and I don't. I see myself as very isolated. Maybe I'm just feeling sorry for myself. But I think I'll go on being lonely until I marry the right man.

My loneliness made me almost panicky when my closest girlfriend, whom I've known since grade school, got married. At the wedding, her parents and other friends came up to me and said: "You're next!" or "When are you getting married?" I felt so terrible. I didn't know what to say and I felt uncomfortable. I wished they hadn't asked me. I feel bad enough anyhow. I see myself always being the single person on such occasions in the future and feeling awkward about it. I hate it. I sometimes think I could survive and not mind it too much if I weren't always reminded how lonely I feel. But people keep asking me why I don't get married.

I'm trying not to sit at home. I tell everyone I'm available to be fixed up. That's the only thing I know to do about it. I don't wait for anybody to come knocking at my door. I try to get out with friends and do things like play tennis and other outside activities. I haven't met anybody I'm interested in. I keep feeling that's the way the future will be too. It's as if I'm doomed to be an old maid, lonely all my life.

In no area of human behavior are our expectations more misleading and potentially frustrating than in our conception of marriage, its meaning, its power to resolve our problems. We see marriage as a panacea to our loneliness. The intimacy of marriage, the commitment to share our life with someone else, can provide a great deal of mutual emotional nourishment. However, this potential is easily contaminated by expectations of what marriage *should* do, what it *should* be like. The most deadly expectation is that love and marriage is a permanent state of being that both people count on, even though there are "the inevitable ups and downs." One way to create loneliness is a "taken-for-granted" attitude, which assumes that because a relationship has culminated in marriage it will be permanent. Like any expectation of an unchanging pattern in human relationships, this attitude is unrealistic and implies that marriage is an insurance policy against loneliness. Many people perceive marriage as a magic wand they can wave; they expect their spouse to provide whatever is needed as a manifestation of his or her love.

Any relationship is an ongoing process. The myth that two people fall in love, marry, and "live happily ever after" sets the stage for a gradual erosion of intimacy and subsequent feelings of loneliness. We know this is a myth, yet on the emotional level we still believe it will never happen to us. We continue to cling to the same old romantic expectations: "Love conquers all . . . especially in marriage."

Even the most stable relationships are constantly evolving. When a marriage or other one-to-one relationship is not nourished by a continuing openness and sharing, the intimacy necessary to sustain a relationship is lost. The toxic patterns that destroy marriages gradually become dominant, and feelings of loneliness begin to emerge. During the peak nourishing periods of a marriage, destructive patterns may seem to be nonexistent but, actually, they are only dormant. When a married couple loses the awareness of their continuing need for self-nourishment and mutual nourishment, deterioration is inevitable.

When we find ourselves feeling lonely despite our existing marital intimacy (and this is surprisingly common), our feelings are often a warning sign that we are failing to realize fully the potential for deterioration present in even the strongest relationship. Nourishing people accept the necessity of an ongoing commitment to provide a continuous flow of love and givingness both to themselves and their partner. The more toxic our attitudes and behavior, the more apt we are to fail to nourish effectively either ourselves or our partner.

> WHEN WE FEEL CHRONICALLY
> LONELY IN MARRIAGE WE NEED TO
> TAKE A HARD LOOK AT THE
> RELATIONSHIP, WHAT WE EXPECT
> FROM IT AND OUR WAY OF BEING
> AND GIVING TO IT.

The commitment to a one-to-one relationship is a commitment to ourselves. It is an attitude, not something that can be measured by material contributions, or words of love, or anything else. In fact, any attempt to measure or compare how we relate to our intimates poisons the essence of what commitment means.

> COMMITMENT IS AN INNER ATTITUDE
> THAT MUST INCLUDE COMPROMISE AS
> AN ESSENTIAL ASPECT OF LOVE.

Gene and Millie had lived together for two years before deciding to marry. Their relationship was rich and nourishing and continued to grow. Their two children were born during the next three years and their relationship grew stronger still.

Both Gene and Millie were busy professionals and, as they each became more successful, the pressure of their work demanded more and more time. Their availability to each other and their children diminished. This was a slow, subtle process, so that neither was aware of what was happening to their relationship. For a while they managed to share time together and with their children on weekends. This too gradually lessened. Occasionally, one would comment about their drifting apart and they would agree to do something about it. Yet they continued to allow other things to take priority, and their intimacy lessened.

By the time their oldest child entered high school, both felt alienated from each other. For all intents and purposes their marriage was dead. They lived together, slept together, even occasionally made love, but the intimacy was almost lost. Their conversation was exemplified by the following:

Millie: How was your day?
Gene: Fine. How was yours?
Millie: Fine.
Gene: That new client accepted my bid and the project will start in a couple of months.
Millie: That's nice. I'm going to attend a seminar next month, and I'll be away for three weeks.
Gene: Well, that sounds exciting.
Millie: Would you like to join me? We could spend a few days together when the conference ends.
Gene: No, I need to tie up a lot of loose ends and do some things that I've been neglecting.
Millie: I have some work to do before I get to the office in the morning.
Gene: I'm a little tired. I think I'll get in bed and read a book.
Millie: Good night, Gene.
Gene: Good night, Millie.

The attitude that a relationship culminating in mutual love can be expected to all but eliminate future loneliness is strongly reinforced by expectations that we have been taught from childhood. Here again the "happily-ever-after" myth takes its deadly toll: "Now that we're married I can relax, for never again will I be lonely since I have found my true love."

Many of us who feel we have a good marriage are frequently bewildered by the intense loneliness we experience in spite of our love relationship. When we live with the expectation that intimacy, especially when it culminates in marriage, means we should no longer feel lonely or unfulfilled, our attitude usually reflects our avoidance of the responsibility to continue to be loving and nourishing both to ourselves and to our spouse. Without this attitude of continuing, active commitment, we are apt to be unaware when emotional inertia slowly sets in, as we begin to take our marriage for granted.

> OUR LONELINESS IS APT TO CONTINUE
> INTO MARRIAGE IF WE LOOK UPON
> MARRIAGE AS A SOLUTION.

The resolution of loneliness is rarely achieved through any relationship, however intimate or deeply involving it might be.

> Casey didn't know he was lonely. He worked hard all day and was exhausted by the time he came home. He would console himself by looking forward to the weekend. He always felt a sense of elation as he drove home from the office Friday afternoon. Yet, something seemed to depress him when he arrived. His expected enjoyment of his family never seemed to materialize. He would walk into the house and find the maid cleaning, the children playing with their friends, and his wife absent.
>
> Sara, Casey's wife, enjoyed many interests. Usually, when she arrived home, the children rushed to her, demanding her attention. Casey watched this drama each Friday. He greeted her with a perfunctory kiss and went back to whatever he was doing while the children vied for her attention. At times he felt resentful, even jealous of the attention they received. He felt as if *he* were waiting for "his turn," and that when the children were finished he would have some time with Sara. Something always hap-

pened before this occurred. Casey felt he was always waiting and usually left unfulfilled.

Casey and Sarah had been married twelve years. It appeared to their friends that they had a solid marriage. They were never seen arguing and seldom quarreled even privately. The family took vacations together every summer. They shared an active social life. Actually, their marriage had been emotionally dead for years. Casey was chronically lonely and knew it. He felt like a fifth wheel with his own family. His attempts to discuss this with Sara met with cursory reassurances: "Of course we all love you." When he persisted in trying to convey his loneliness, Sara would get irritated and accuse him of being in a bad mood.

About two years later Casey packed a bag and told Sara that he was leaving, he was in love with another woman and wanted a divorce. Shortly after he left, Sara realized that she had shared little intimacy with her husband for a long time. She had taken their marriage for granted. She asked, even begged Casey for another chance. He was truly saddened by her request, but angry as well. Without blaming her or himself, he told Sara that it was too late. His love for her had died from frustration, loneliness, and starvation.

Many people are perplexed that, despite their long-standing intimate relationships, they nevertheless suffer from chronic loneliness. This reflects the unrealistic expectation that a nourishing, intimate relationship, particularly when it includes marriage and children, is automatically self-sustaining and should alleviate any feelings of loneliness.

MARRIAGE IS NOT A WAY OF LIFE. IT IS A RELATIONSHIP.

Expectations lead to the erosion of any relationship. The myth that the resolution of loneliness will result because we have found an intimate one-to-one relationship is a cop-out. It begins a toxic process which dissipates the mutual nourishment that occurs when both people are committed to sustaining nourishing interaction *and* growth of their separate selves.

The traditional attitude that marriage is a solution to our emotional problems actually nurtures loneliness and eventually will lead to despair and/or divorce. We poison ourselves whenever we expect more out of a marriage than we actually experience and then feel cheated. In most such instances, instead of looking within ourselves for the resolution of our frustrations, we blame our mate and persist in focusing our efforts on manipulating our spouse into satisfying our needs. This is one of the principal patterns of *creating* loneliness in marriage.

Another common pattern of generating loneliness is to cling to the fantasy that a marriage that doesn't resolve our loneliness is a bad marriage and that a different, "better" relationship will do the trick. "I'll get a divorce and try someone else." Or: "I'll have an affair that will give me what I'm not getting at home." The problem in these externally directed solutions is that we are most apt to bring our old toxic attitudes and behavior patterns into each new relationship. Without greater awareness the results will be the same.

Peggy awoke at seven on a quiet Sunday morning. The night before, she had been apprehensive that this would be a difficult day. Her plans with friends had been cancelled. She had hoped to sleep late so that the day would not seem so long. She made some coffee, smoked a cigarette, and turned on the television, but there was nothing of interest. She thumbed through some magazines, quickly felt bored, and threw them on the floor in exasperation. What was she going to do to kill the day? Whom could she call? Anything was better than the prospect of spending the whole day alone. She chain-smoked as she paced her living room. The apartment needed cleaning, but somehow she didn't feel like it. There was correspondence to catch up on, but that also seemed blah. She called a few of her friends, but they were all busy.

By noon, Peggy was depressed. She threw herself on the bed and began sobbing. She felt terribly lonely and didn't know what to do about it. She ran out of cigarettes and went to the market. It seemed as if everyone in the market was with someone else. She felt intense depression and loneliness each time she saw a couple together. If only she had a man, she thought, she wouldn't be in this dilemma, and she hurried home, since her tears were already beginning to flow. She set the groceries in the kitchen, sat down, and cried for what seemed like hours.

Peggy is chronically lonely and for years has been all too aware of her dread of solitude. During the week she lost herself in work, came home, had a drink, made dinner and relaxed for a while before going to bed. Other nights she attended classes or went out with girlfriends for dinner or a movie.

Whatever Peggy did, whatever friendships she enjoyed, she still insisted that the only real solution to her loneliness was an intimate relationship with a man. She was twenty-eight, divorced for three years, and had had two affairs, each lasting a year. These relationships were frustrating and painful because the emotional depth she longed for never developed. Lately, her Sunday loneliness had become more frequent. She dreaded the weekends and looked forward to Mondays when she could lose herself in the weekly routine.

Her growing despair culminated in an attempted suicide, after which she began therapy. She had felt that the whole resolution to her loneliness depended almost entirely on establishing a meaningful relationship that would lead to marriage.

In therapy she became aware of the enormous burden of expectations she placed on men. She realized how she had placed the responsibility for her loneliness first on her ex-husband and then on each of her subsequent lovers. She also saw her own lack of giving in these relationships, as she secretly withheld herself while waiting for expectations to be fulfilled. She began to see more of her own toxic patterns, how she used friends and activities to avoid her loneliness, thus failing to appreciate them for their own value. Lastly, she saw how *she* had narrowed her world in so many ways by refusing to explore her own potential. There was little left for her but loneliness.

Peggy's case exemplifies how we perpetuate our loneliness by insisting on a single requirement (in her case marriage) and become even more likely to enhance our loneliness searching for the answer "out there." It is for this reason that we tend to have a series of bad marriages or disappointing relationships. Yet we may continue to insist blindly that it's because the "right person" still hasn't come along!

12

How Not to Be Lonely
in a Crowd

The loneliness and sense of alienation that is so prevalent in our society as a whole is a manifestation of the same attitudes and behavior with which we create and perpetuate our personal loneliness. We rarely notice how we as a society continuously perpetuate an atmosphere that breeds loneliness. For example, we are taught to value rugged individualism, independence, and freedom, while an open expression of emotional needs is often considered a sign of weakness. We tend to carry these societal attitudes into our personal lives and thereby lose our perspective. We confuse individualism and self-reliance with the notion that we should be able to get along without really needing anyone in our personal lives. Then we transmit this attitude to each other.

The principal way society teaches us to resolve our emotional needs or conflicts is to suppress them and strive for success. Early on, we are indoctrinated with the belief that life is a game in which the "winners" get all the goodies and the losers, which means the vast majority of us, ought to feel ashamed for "failing." The main thing is to learn how to compete successfully. This attitude continually pits us against each other. Then we wonder why so many of us are lonely, or why our cities vibrate with hostility and anger, and why we are so fearful of being victimized by other people's aspirations: emotional, financial, sexual, or otherwise.

It is ironic that success is of little value in resolving loneliness, while, on the other hand, when we feel we haven't been successful, we blame our loneliness on our failure. We become more obsessed with our drive to become successful and often less concerned about how we relate to ourselves and others. For those who succeed, their unfulfilled expectations create a shattering disappointment which is usually too embarrassing to share.

Try looking into the faces of "successful" people. See for yourself if they genuinely appear happy.

> SUCCESS MAKES A GREAT CAMOUFLAGE
> TO CONCEAL LONELINESS.

In the world of achievers, it is socially taboo to reveal one's needs. Wealth or influence offers an excellent hiding place for chronic loneliness. The real meaning of the success of others can easily fool us even about those we are most intimate with.

Usually, as we go about our daily activities, we are aloof, withdrawn, or preoccupied with the business at hand. If we try walking down the street radiating a smile and making eye contact with strangers, we will usually be ignored. Otherwise, more often than not, we will be met with suspicion (largely focused on anxiety that ours is some kind of sexual approach) or even hostility.

> SEEKING OPEN CONTACT WITH
> OTHERS IN OUR ALIENATED SOCIETY
> OFTEN EVOKES FEELINGS OF THREAT.

Despite our society's approval of independence, self-reliance, and successful competition, these fail dismally to replace the needed contact and a feeling of being accepted and loved for ourselves, and not for our accomplishments or other outstanding attributes.

When the facades we have created to counter our phobias are ripped away, for example, by some dramatic incident, the latent need for openness and sharing bursts forth. An accident or fire typically overwhelms our self-consciousness and we begin to speak to each other in a manner which we would otherwise never dare. Unfortunately, most of us quickly return to our isolated, alienated attitudes once the crisis is over.

Compassion goes out the window when we fail to recognize that we all share many of the same fears, anxieties, hopes, and aspirations. A communal feeling toward others will always exist on the deepest level, even though we are so frightened of it that we avoid our awareness of it.

When we totally commit ourselves to "success," whether it has been achieved or whether we are still striving for it, we are lost on a detour that leads only to chronic loneliness. The sooner we recognize that it is an illusion that success will bring us the answer to our emotional pain and deprivation, the sooner we can embark on our search for new, more fruitful pathways away from loneliness.

Developing our own sense of communality, compassion, and awareness of others, and being willing to show it openly, creates infinite possibilities for more sharing and nourishing relations. This kind of social attitude offers us a far more fertile field in which to resolve our loneliness. There is nothing to work through, nothing to analyze, nothing to understand in this process. Any imagined "prerequisites" to prove ourselves first are only more ways of avoiding the fantasized catastrophes we imagine will occur if we risk being more open about our personal fears and emotional needs.

As our individual identities fade into computer banks, personal warmth and friendly relating to others becomes more difficult.

> IN OUR SOCIETY A WORKING ADULT
> NEEDS NO PERSONAL RELATIONSHIPS
> WITH OTHERS IN ORDER TO SURVIVE
> PHYSICALLY.

In contrast, people in so-called primitive societies, in which most time and energy is utilized for physical survival, are naturally bound by a mutual dependency which fosters more personal and intimate contact among them.

Our society teaches us many myths which foster alienation

and loss of identity. It is now popular to believe that achievement, social approval, material success, sex appeal, and so forth will provide a resolution to inner loneliness. These social myths imply that success will enhance the likelihood of bringing more love into our lives.

> NO AMOUNT OF EXTERNAL SUCCESS
> EVER OFFSETS THE LACK OF AN INNER
> FEELING OF SELF-LOVE AND
> SELF-ACCEPTANCE.

Our self-image is too often dominated by other people's responsiveness, or the lack of it, to what we have accomplished. While we may feel nourished by receiving approval and recognition, they become a trap when considered of primary importance.

Financial success, for example, is a carrot that society dangles in front of us, promising an end to emotional frustrations and deprivation. When we feel we haven't succeeded, we may sincerely believe that wealthy or powerful people surely have no problems with loneliness or feelings of isolation. This illusion readily becomes an insidious and deadly trap, since success is, by definition, limited to a relatively few people.

Drugs and Alcohol: The Hallmarks of Alienation

Use of drugs (prescription as well as illegal drugs) and alcohol is by far the most common method of alleviating feelings of loneliness.

> Evelyn was a legal secretary who considered herself a social failure. She was an alcoholic, but her drinking did not interfere with her job or other activities. Before dinner she would begin to drink and gradually become intoxicated as the evening progressed. She had been lonely most of her life and found that alcohol relieved her pain. When she was drinking she became more lighthearted and spontaneous; otherwise she usually felt inhibited and depressed.

She had been married to Larry for ten years. In spite of his constant reassurance of his love, she feared he would lose interest as she grew older. Alcohol enabled her to act like the kind of woman she imagined Larry wanted. Actually, while he enjoyed her lighthearted, frivolous behavior, he also appreciated her quietness. Yet Evelyn was afraid to risk being herself without the use of alcohol. She had a self-rejecting, unloving attitude toward herself that is so characteristic of the chronically lonely.

Their sex life was good, yet she feared she was not passionate enough and had gnawing doubts about Larry's satisfaction. Again, she was unable to accept his reassurance. Whenever Larry seemed in a romantic mood, Evelyn would drink more than usual in order to be the kind of sex partner she imagined he desired.

Many people, including Larry, had jokingly commented that: "Evelyn is really a different person when she's had a couple of drinks." While such statements were intended as compliments, they only enhanced her anxiety and long-standing fear that others, especially Larry, would see how unlovable she was underneath. To her, such remarks meant that her "real self," her sober personality, was inadequate.

The use of drugs and alcohol is a socially sanctioned way to induce an artificial solution to loneliness and to anesthetize us against emotional pain. In the long run this only hampers our ability to cope with loneliness and makes the discovery of effective resolutions much more difficult.

When we use drugs or alcohol to counteract our fears and anxieties, we know only too well that something artificial is affecting our way of relating. This fact we usually avoid or rationalize. ("I'll only use them when I'm going to be with someone I'm particularly interested in and until we get to know each other better.") In the long run, such "benefits" are far outweighed by the sense of isolation they create. The more dependent we become on them, the more our real selves are distorted or hidden from others and, to a considerable extent, from ourselves, as well. Our capacity for intimacy has been drugged.

Drugs and alcohol avoid the risky business of self-disclosure. The false sense of bravado, courage, or openness may indeed have its rewards, but it doesn't fool us about our loneliness. The fear of being "found out" increases our anxieties and, in turn, our dependency. We may never take the risk of finding out how the world would react to our natural selves. For example, when we have been lonely for some period of time, we also feel an intense urgency to relate successfully, which, of course, intensifies our apprehension and fear of failure. In such instances it is generally socially sanctioned to use a drug or alcohol to bring at least temporary relief. If we are "successful" in establishing a good relationship, then there is always the question of how much our "success" comes from inside us and how much arises from our anesthesias and "turn-ons."

Drugs and alcohol are a major source of self-perpetuated loneliness. They are sanctioned, or at least tolerated, by practically every segment of society. The implied attitude of society is that if you can stay out of trouble and if you can afford it, a drug or alcohol habit is acceptable.

Conclusion

Derogating society has become popular. There is no dearth of valid criticism about the many toxic aspects of the society in which we live. However, when we convince ourselves that we are helpless to do anything about our loneliness (it's not my fault, it's "them") and turn society into a scapegoat, it becomes all too easy to put the blame *there* and to wallow impotently in our anger and frustration. This is simply another avoidance of responsibility for our loneliness. We are our society; each of us not only feels this sense of alienation to some degree, but, in addition, we probably contribute to it, whether we are aware of it or not.

EACH OF US CREATES HIS OR HER
OWN ATTITUDES ABOUT SOCIETY.
HIDING BEHIND THE SMOKESCREEN

THAT "NOBODY CARES" ONLY
ENHANCES OUR FEELINGS OF
ALIENATION.

While we have available to us an enormous range of life-styles, we can carry our loneliness with us wherever we go and whatever mode of living we adopt. We will continue to be lonely until we acknowledge that the problem is not "out there," but within ourselves.

If we seek love, there are people everywhere who are loving and available. But this concept is meaningless unless we are willing to risk being open and to reach out for what we want, *despite* the rejections we fear. We need not use feelings of rejection as an excuse to avoid moving on and continuing our search.

IN OUR ALIENATED SOCIETY ALL OF
US ARE APT TO BE PARANOID TO
SOME DEGREE. THE CHRONICALLY
LONELY HAVE NO MONOPOLY ON
UNREALISTIC SUSPICION.

Any rationalization or excuse we use to build a case for the difficulty of establishing emotionally gratifying relationships within the structure of our existing society is only another kind of cop-out.

WHETHER WE ARE AWARE OF IT OR
NOT, THE *NEED* TO LOVE AND THE
NEED TO GIVE EXIST WITHIN ALL OF
US.

Love is a feeling of caring that goes beyond our needs for personal gratification. This means our relations within our community reflect our need to give to others because we care. PERIOD.

A FEELING OF BELONGING AND LOVE
TOWARD ALL OF HUMANKIND IS THE
BEST ANTIDOTE IN RESOLVING
LONELINESS ON THE SOCIAL LEVEL.
WE MUST BREAK OUT OF THE

PARANOID "ME AGAINST THEM"
ATTITUDE SO STRONGLY ENCOURAGED
BY OUR COMPETITIVE SUCCESS-
ORIENTED SOCIETY. EVEN IN AN
ALIENATED SOCIETY, THE WAY TO
FEEL LOVED IS TO LOVE. THE WAY
TO FEEL CARED FOR IS TO CARE.

13

❧❧❧❧❧❧

The Beginning of the
End of Fear

The fears and anxieties about death and dying are the most powerful and ominous phobias in our culture. Most of us view death as the ultimate state of loneliness. Our attitudes toward death are a direct reflection of our attitudes toward life. When our primary attitude has been a sense of satisfaction with our lives, we are more willing and, for some, more ready to accept death.

If we have lived a life of chronic loneliness and feel lost in our struggle to find meaningfulness and satisfaction in our lives, our anxiety about death is apt to be greater. This is true even when, as is often the case, we see death as a release from our unhappiness. Regardless of our age, everything feels unfinished.

> WHEN WE LIVE A LONELY LIFE WE
> ARE APT TO MAKE DEATH INTO THE
> SYMBOL OF ULTIMATE LONELINESS.

Preoccupation with death is toxic and literally drains the life out of us. It robs us of our existence in the present and our ability to live life to the fullest. Similarly, thoughts of death only enhance our preoccupation with past regrets and fears of future loneliness.

> DEATH CAN BE VIEWED IN A
> NOURISHING OR TOXIC FASHION. ONCE

WE REALLY ACCEPT ITS INEVITABILITY
IT CAN BE A POWERFUL MOTIVATION
FOR LIVING IN AND EXPERIENCING
THE RICHNESS OF THE PRESENT.

Death, if we see it as the epitome of loneliness, is most effectively dealt with in the present. Acceptance of death can free us to strive for fuller awareness and to experience life. We begin dying the moment we are born, and when we live in the present we are continuously reborn each time our consciousness expands and our potential is actualized.

"Sit down," said the doctor. His words seemed to come to Mary Jo as if from somewhere else. She was in a mild state of shock. She remembered saying something about wanting to know everything. Some of his words still rang in her ears: "cancer" . . . "about six months" . . . "inoperable" . . . "new drugs" . . . "highly experimental."

As she returned home and closed the door to her apartment it finally hit her. She had leukemia and she was going to die.

Mary Jo was thirty-six. She had lived alone for five years after her divorce. She had always struggled with loneliness, but in the past year she had finally come to enjoy her life and found it so fulfilling that her loneliness seemed to be part of another lifetime. She was dedicated to her profession as a physical therapist working with handicapped children. Tennis and skiing were her outside interests. There was never enough time for her to have her fill of either activity. Most of her friends were similarly involved in one or both sports. The result was a social life that was as busy as she chose. Several of the men she played tennis with were current or ex-lovers. In general, Mary Jo found life meaningful and fulfilling and she was grateful for having so many exciting options to choose among.

When she entered the hospital for treatment and further evaluation, she used the time to contemplate her dilemma. She was afraid she would begin to feel sorry for herself and become obsessed with torturous fantasies. She recalled how her aunt, who had died of cancer several years before, had lived in terror for two years. Even at the time, Mary Jo wondered if her aunt's agony weren't as attributable to her mental attitude as to the disease itself.

As the months went by, Mary Jo worked intensely with herself. She summoned her fortitude and courage to accept reality without allowing herself to collapse into depression. She was determined not to burden those who cared about her by complaining to them. She had seen how her aunt had done this until the entire family and her closest friends suffered to such an extent that being in her presence became exhausting.

Mary Jo had not considered herself a religious person. She had little formal religious training during her childhood and had never joined a church. Yet a deep spiritual awakening now arrived of its own accord and provided her with a sense of peace and often a sense of joy that were astonishing to her. She found herself praying to God.

After she left the hospital she was able to resume work. While first she had felt weak, he strength gradually returned almost to normal. The doctors told her that she was in a state of remission from her leukemia. While they could not predict how long this would continue, everyone felt encouraged. Mary Jo was grateful and determined to make the most of it. She had no interest in doing anything different. At times, before she became ill, she had fantasized that if she ever learned that she had but a short time to live, she would use all her savings and travel around the world as long as she could. Such thoughts now seemed superficial to her. Her appreciation of the ordinary experiences she had always taken for granted seemed unbelievably rich and exciting. She was living and experiencing everything with a far fuller awareness than she had ever known. But her new awareness was overshadowed by the joy she experienced in being with others. Never had she appreciated her friends and loved ones as she did now.

It is now three years since Mary Jo first learned that she had leukemia. While she has had relapses that necessitated further hospitalization, each time she has gone into remission subsequently. Her life, aside from the fact she no longer engages in strenuous physical activity, is fairly normal. No one can predict at this time what the course of her illness will be.

It may be difficult for most of us to understand that Mary Jo has come to terms with the possibility of her imminent death to such an extent that it is of secondary importance to her extraordinary appreciation of life. She knows on a deeper level than most of us that we are all, in a sense, continuously living "at death's door." She truly doesn't see any difference between her life now and the lives of those around her. Only a couple of her friends believed her and knew what she meant when she said: "What's the use of any of us worrying about death since it's inevitable anyhow!"

Our society is so phobic about death that acceptance of it is, for most of us, extremely difficult. Yet there are many who accept death and, even when they know it is imminent, continue to enjoy a full life, moment by moment, without bitterness, fear, or anger. They do not make deals or try to manipulate. (Doctor, keep me alive no matter what you have to do!) Instead, they accept the aloneness (not loneliness) that is, to some extent, an unavoidable aspect of dying. With this attitude comes the release of enormous energy otherwise lost in trying to deny death or in living in dread of it.

A fuller, more creative, joyful life is likely for each of us when we face the need to reconcile ourselves to death. Acceptance of death enhances our ability to experience our lives to the fullest without the enormous burden we place on ourselves when we continue our preoccupation with death and thereby add an additional element to our self-induced loneliness.

The lonelier we feel, the more frightened we become about the inevitability of death and the more we become increasingly fearful. The death of a loved one is often as difficult for us to become reconciled to as our own death. When we have lived in chronic loneliness, the death of a loved one becomes a kind of emotional bankruptcy in which our "investment"—love, time, and energy—is suddenly lost to us. While we have appreciated the lost love, this response suggests that we tried to make the relationship a safeguard against loneliness.

The more totally we love, the easier it is to let go. This does not imply that we can avoid the pain of mourning but, rather, that we can be aware that the lonelier we are, the more we want to hang onto those we love. As we learn how to break out of our loneliness, we also learn how to hold our loved ones with an open hand rather than clutching at them as if they were a possession. The same process occurs within ourselves: the more we break out of the patterns with which we continue to make ourselves lonely, the easier it becomes to accept our own death.

> ### THERE ARE NO GUARANTEES IN LIFE, ONLY OPPORTUNITIES.

When we are lost in our loneliness, we are unwilling to accept the possibility that at any moment we, or a loved one, may be taken away by death. Intellectually, we know this, but few of us accept it emotionally. Clinging to our fear of death is detrimental to our experience of nourishment and joy in the present.

14

~~~~~~~~

Living in the World of Now

Understanding *what* we do to perpetuate our loneliness and *how* we do it provides all the clues we need to discover effective antidotes. The continuous awareness of *what* our personal patterns of self-induced loneliness are and how we manifest these in relating to ourselves and others is always the starting point for breaking out of our loneliness. The more clearly we see how our attitudes and behavior can deprive us and others of the emotional nourishment we all need, the stronger our determination to give them up will become. As nourishing kinds of experiences increase, loneliness fades into the background, and our preoccupation with it and fear of it steadily loses power and gradually becomes obsolete.

This process of awareness of underlying attitudes that have actively sustained and fostered our loneliness often brings a growing insight into how we can experiment with new, different attitudes and behavior. Experimentation is the unavoidable risk-taking process. It involves new learning based on the new experiences that occur when we are ready to take risks. We learn how to utilize inner resources we may not have even known existed within us. When we discover these latent potentials, vast new possibilities arise for learning how to use them to break out of our patterns of self-induced loneliness.

This awareness and self-confrontation are not magical nor will they bring instant relief. Usually, when we have a history of loneliness, we have allowed ourselves to be victimized by the false hope of quick or other painless gimmicks. The immediate effect of becoming aware of toxic patterns usually includes both a feeling of hope *and* apprehension about breaking out of the facades, manipulations, and avoidances, which, while extremely toxic, provide the comfort of the familiar and to some degree have been effective anesthesias against the emotional pain of our loneliness.

When we see the simplicity and freedom of greater openness and honesty, it can fill us with the excitement that comes with discovering the possibilities of new, more nourishing, more effective solutions. Still, our old fears and self-doubts are likely to continue generating feelings of insecurity and fear of failure. Thus all antidote processes can be seen as part of our personal growth and evolution, in which we struggle to use our new learning and awareness to break out of obsolete attitudes and the behavior in which they are reflected.

Because of the continuing emergence of our habitual self-poisoning patterns, it is essential that we make a commitment to the antidote *process*. To take the attitude: "I'll try it and see if it works" is to abort the antidote at the outset.

> WHATEVER PATHWAYS WE CHOOSE
> AWAY FROM LONELINESS, THESE MUST
> EVENTUALLY MAKE MORE SENSE TO US
> THAN THE OLD PATTERNS THEY
> REPLACE.

Part of this new learning process calls for a continuing commitment to be aware of how our newer, experimental attitudes and behavior affect the quality of our lives. This essential awareness tells us on a gut level whether we are on a more meaningful path away from loneliness or whether we are simply on another detour that will eventually only leave us returning for more loneliness. The basic antidote process of continual awareness of how we experience what we do breaks the illusion most people have: that if we do what we have been told to do and do it well enough, we will receive our reward—in this case, the resolution of our loneliness. The opposite attitude is far more realistic:

THE MOST ESSENTIAL CRITERION IN
DECIDING WHAT IS NOURISHING OR
TOXIC IS HOW WE PERSONALLY
EXPERIENCE A PARTICULAR ATTITUDE
OR BEHAVIOR PATTERN.

This is the essence of what it means to function as our own person in the present. When we have lost ourselves in loneliness, it may initially feel like blind groping because when we become aware of an old negative pattern and have been able to break out of it, a new, more effective pattern does not instantly emerge to take its place. Nevertheless, the best we can do at the moment is to break out of these obsolete patterns and the emotional stagnation they invariably create. In the continuously unfolding present, breaking out creates a psychic space, an emptiness that could be referred to as a "fertile void," a state of openness that establishes the optimum conditions for the emergence of the new, more nourishing attitudes and behavior that can become the antidotes to chronic loneliness. New awareness and insights will begin to fill this void, *provided* we have the patience and self-trust to tolerate the temporary anxiety that comes with the uncertainty and lack of structure we feel.

All games of loneliness are circular and unending and do not lead to any creative resolution. Each is a manifestation of the way we avoid and distract ourselves in our efforts to escape significant confrontations with our fear of loneliness and our anxiety about taking responsibility for creating it. This is why we may cling to these games so tenaciously even when we know how destructive they are. They serve as psychic tranquilizers that dull our awareness of how we create our loneliness.

We may react with intense anxiety if circumstances interfere with our usual games of avoidance. For example, the business person who escapes loneliness by staying lost in a steady stream of ventures becomes irritable, bored, or restless when vacationing. Often these feelings are symptoms of deep loneliness. Or, if it is pointed out to a lonely person that he or she constantly criticizes others, such comments may be met with indignation, anger, and, of course, criticism.

> THE MOST IMPORTANT ANTIDOTE TO
> OUR LONELINESS IS THE WILLINGNESS
> TO TAKE A GOOD LOOK AT HOW WE
> RELATE TO OURSELVES AND OTHERS.

Since breaking out of old behavior patterns and attitudes, even when they are recognized as toxic, elicits the anxiety most of us experience when we are in new, unfamiliar territory without our usual psychological support system, there is no easy way out. The breaking out of what we now see as obsolete or self-destructive patterns is usually the most difficult, and the most essential, aspect of any antidote that involves discovering new and different possibilities of resolving our loneliness.

Nonjudgmental awareness of the games with which we create and sustain our loneliness is most valuable because, while they are obsolete now, they have been the best we were able to do in the past. Even when we are extremely self-destructive, we always do the best we can for ourselves. When we take a judgmental or derogatory attitude toward obsolete, toxic patterns (e.g., "Why didn't I see that sooner?"), we create a new toxic pattern.

> WE CAN BEST SAY GOOD-BYE TO OUR
> PATTERNS OF LONELINESS BY
> ACCEPTING WITHOUT CONDEMNATION
> THAT WE JUST DON'T NEED THEM ANY
> MORE.

When we become aware of our games of self-induced loneliness and wish to have a nourishing attitude toward them, then we do not criticize ourselves for having them. Furthermore, we make no resolutions about giving them up. Instead, the beginning of the antidote process is to become as fully aware as possible that at the moment these *are* part of our self. This is the beginning of the self-trusting attitude which will lead to evolution and growth toward new attitudes and behavior patterns that are more fulfilling.

Seeing what we are doing, becoming fully aware of poisonous consequences, is a confrontation with the self that leads to an increasing determination to do something more effective. This is the source of the motivating energy necessary for change and growth. Rebuking ourselves is always destructive and does not elicit the motivation necessary for change. The newly discovered awareness of our toxic patterns is painful, and this pain is necessary for change. This gut-level pain, feeling that one has had enough, is both the necessary and sufficient source for the motivation to risk experimentation.

In contrast, the declaration that: "Now that I see my games of loneliness, I am going to give them up," usually turns out to be little more than a well-intended "New Year's resolution," rather than a commitment to a process.

EFFECTIVE ANTIDOTES ARE FOUND IN THE CONTINUOUS EMERGENCE OF THE INNER NOURISHING SELF, WHICH NATURALLY UNFOLDS WHEN WE STOP INTERRUPTING IT.

We have said that it is characteristic, when we feel chronically lonely, to stubbornly persist in looking for an easy, permanent solution. We may try one thing after another, hoping that we will finally find *the* answer. The pain of these endless, futile endeavors, and the wasted energy, may become as destructive as our loneliness. Each false start, each "quick cure" turns into another disappointment that leaves us feeling more futile than ever. The list of these available "cures" is so extensive that we could spend a lifetime experimenting and still not have tried them all.

When the pain of loneliness is intense enough and is not temporarily dissipated through these well-intended false starts, the pain itself becomes the motivational force necessary to initiate and persist in the more nourishing processes which offer far greater possibilities for the resolution of loneliness.

> SUFFICIENT PSYCHIC PAIN IS A
> PREREQUISITE TO TAKING THE
> NECESSARY RISKS INVOLVED IN
> ATTEMPTING A MORE REALISTIC
> APPROACH TO RESOLVING OUR
> LONELINESS.

Since loneliness is a process, feelings of loneliness will vary widely at different times. Similarly, all antidotes are processes, so that their nourishing effects, their ability to alleviate the pain of our loneliness, may begin immediately and gradually become more effective with a few ups and downs along the way.

> ANTIDOTES FOR CHRONIC LONELINESS
> ARE FOR THE MOST PART SIMPLE. AND
> THEY ARE NOT EASY.

When we embark on our chosen pathways away from loneliness the pain gradually lessens as new, more gratifying experiences occur. However, this evolution cannot be programmed or scheduled. Rather, all antidotes call for a continuing commitment to appropriate processes. We of course choose those antidotes that seem to make the most sense and seem most applicable to us; this means we *also* must change our antidote patterns as this seems warranted. Since breaking out of loneliness is always a process of growth and inner change, our perception of the most suitable antidotes also changes. With our personal evolution comes a greater ability to discriminate among the many antidote patterns. The choice of antidote is a manifestation of our growth process.

Getting Started

Since at times a particular antidote may seem very effective and also elicit intense anxiety, our tendency may be to abandon this approach and try others that seem less threatening. In such instances, the awareness that we are shifting antidotes on the basis of anxiety is critical. Detours away from the resolution of our loneliness are apt to occur if we are unaware that our choice of antidotes is based on selecting those that are less painful, even though they may be less effective. For example, we may discover that the more threatening antidote is really the most effective approach only *after* we have let go of it and turned to other approaches that cause us less anxiety. This new awareness calls for a new confrontation with ourselves to see if (or when) we are willing to resume giving top priority to what again seems to be the most effective approach even though it may still be the most painful or threatening.

Since we all hope for quick results the idea of a continuing *process* of developing antidotes may cause us to feel pessimistic. We may anticipate an ordeal that evokes feelings of futility even before we have begun. This reflects a basic attitude which undoubtedly has contributed significantly to our past loneliness. It means we are still oriented toward finding easy, fast answers. Once we recognize the unrealistic nature of this model, we begin the process of confronting reality and taking an important step toward the resolution of loneliness.

Putting Ourselves Back Together

One of the effects of chronic loneliness is a gradual fragmentation of our self. We block, disown, or renounce various aspects of our identity which create too much anxiety. For example, we may have learned in childhood to be docile and "nice to everybody" because our parents punished us whenever we became angry. This fragmentation continues to limit the scope of our awareness so that we avoid perceiving whatever is too threatening, in this case, expressing our anger.

THE MORE FRAGMENTED WE ARE, THE LESS CAPABLE WE ARE OF REACTING FULLY TO OUR CURRENT EXPERIENCES AS THEY OCCUR.

Fragmentation actually makes us less able to learn about ourselves and others. Our perception of the world is increasingly narrowed and distorted the more fragmented we are. For example, some lonely people really don't see how they turn people off, while to everyone else it is obvious. This is mainly because their ability to perceive the effects of their attitudes has been lost, i.e., fragmented. Through awareness of the effects of our reacting, we normally discover what is nourishing and what is toxic, and respond accordingly. One of the effects of chronic loneliness is that these feelings, emotions, and other reactions to the normal awareness process are blocked. Essential experiential data which tells us what is going on *now* is not perceived or integrated. New learning is impossible. Such fragmentations prevent us from functioning without the total inner resources which are available to us. Our actions and responsiveness, how we relate to our inner self and the outer world, become increasingly ineffective as this fragmentation process intensifies.

Centering

"Centering" is the antidote process with which we can integrate ourselves. Centering involves a conscious effort to pay attention by focusing on *all* sensory and perceptual data that is available at any moment. We become particularly aware of any tendencies to reject data that is threatening or out of harmony with our preconceived ideas.

Centering is a "broad-spectrum" antidote against the poisonous attitudes and behavior patterns that lead to isolation, alienation, and loneliness. Since it enables us to focus our attention on our perceptions and awareness, it is also the most critical attitude in discerning manipulative attempts by others. We learn to trust our own experience of others far more than anyone else's impressions. In contrast, when we are lonely, we tend to give away our center (and our power) to someone else; we become externally oriented. Our center is outside of ourself. We tend to believe others rather than ourselves. When we are in doubt, and this is usually the case, we believe others know better than we do. Whenever we lose our center, we give away our personal power and ability to learn how to take responsibility for our own lives. When we are centered, we have accepted that the best we can do is to take responsibility for ourselves, to trust our inner voice and our own intuitive reactions as our most valid source of wisdom.

We usually experience both negative and positive feelings about the possibilities of a nourishing encounter with another person. These fixed messages are often interpreted as a malfunction within ourselves. We may even resent any negative feeling ("bad vibes") as a hindrance to a relationship we very much hope will flourish, and we may actively push them away. In so doing, we again fragment our own perceptual experience. The unhappy encounters that victimize us when we are lonely are often manifestations of this fragmentation of sensory data into what we want to see and what we want to ignore.

When we find ourselves blaming our feelings of loneliness on a lack of intimate relationships, we are apt to limit the area of our exploration. For example, we may pay attention only to our intimate sexual relationships. In the following case, Harry learned a great deal about the reasons he so frequently found himself the victim of one-way relationships when he became aware of what happened in an ill-fated business venture he undertook with a new partner.

Harry met Bill at a convention and they became friends when they discovered they were from the same city. Both were specialists in real estate management and seemed to have similar views on the subject. Bill suggested that they might work well together and they agreed to start their own company. Three months later they opened.

Harry had always wanted to be in business for himself and, while he felt confident that he and Bill could make a go of it together, there was something about Bill that made Harry uneasy. These feelings he sloughed off as anxiety about his new venture.

Gradually his uneasiness grew until he could no longer avoid it. Their company had prospered and Bill began to arrive at the office later and later. Now Harry began to take a good look at the uneasiness he had felt since the beginning of their association. Bill was constantly using excuses in order to get Harry to handle more of the work, while Bill seemed always to be rushing off to check out some vague project or a "possible new client" that rarely materialized.

It was when Bill announced that he had bought a new home in an area that was a two-hour drive from their office that Harry finally faced up to his mistake in choosing a partner. Now it was clear to Harry that Bill had never held up his half of the partnership. Each time he had confronted Bill about the lopsided nature of their workloads, Bill had somehow managed to convince him that the arrangement was fair, that Harry was splitting hairs, or that he would make it up to him later.

It was three years before Harry finally took the action he could have taken much earlier if he had paid attention to the message of his own feelings. In retrospect, it was amazing to him that he could have blinded himself to the obvious for so long.

The whole experience broadened Harry's awareness of his personal relations. In his love life, as well as in friendships, he became aware of how he had focused too narrowly on whether he and others had similar "personalities" that would lead to compatible relationships. Now he realized that: "Many of my relationships where I thought the other person and myself had a lot in common were doomed from the beginning. I didn't want to see how often other people wanted to take advantage of me or use me in some way."

All of us have been disappointed by relationships. We may become aware that there were negative feelings experienced early in the relationship, but for our own reasons we chose to ignore them and thereby created more emotional pain for ourselves. This kind of "ostrich game" doesn't change reality. The negative aspects that we refuse to confront at the beginning of a relationship only become more destructive the longer we try to ignore them.

When loneliness makes us exceptionally vulnerable to toxic relationships, it is particularly important that we are all aware of the value of *all* of the varying cues and messages we receive, especially those that are not in harmony with our needs, recognizing the conflict and ambivalence which exist in all relationships and remaining continually aware of both the nourishing and toxic aspects of our relationships from the beginning.

When we do not victimize ourselves with our loneliness by shutting off what we don't want to see, sooner or later our confusion or conflict will crystallize and provide us with a more complete picture of the nourishing and destructive potentials in the relationship. When we trust ourselves, we will find that our own spontaneous flow of awareness will guide us and also provide the best insurance against any tendency to fall back into fragmenting ourselves by refusing to see what it is.

Letting Go of Our Expectations

As we discussed earlier, when we are lonely, we tend to look to others as our primary source of nourishment. This sets the stage for the many kinds of expectations we are then apt to place on others.

EXPECTATIONS ARE THE MOST
COMMON WAY OF POISONING ANY
RELATIONSHIP.

When our focus is strongly set on finding other people who will satisfy our feelings of emotional deprivation, we may find it difficult to accept the limits of their willingness or ability to give. When we are lonely, we are less likely to risk initiating the loving, caring attitude toward others that we would like for ourselves, with no expectation that they should respond to us in the same manner.

THE ATTITUDE OF NO EXPECTATIONS,
THAT NO ONE OWES US ANYTHING,
CAN IN ITSELF FREE US TO DISCOVER
NEW PATHWAYS FROM LONELINESS.

This is the prime attitude necessary for a new confrontation. We then take full responsibility for our loneliness and acknowledge that, in intimate relating, nobody owes us anything. A new commitment emerges, in which we are now willing to cope with our loneliness from within ourselves, using our own resources, rather than continuing our manipulation of others or hoping someone else will rescue us. This shift in attitude also facilitates a greater willingness to tolerate the pain of loneliness rather than clinging to our old games and thereby continuing to contaminate our new relationships.

Expectations prevent us from taking full responsibility for seeking and sustaining those relationships that are mutually loving and giving and from breaking out of those that aren't. There are, of course, no guarantees that any of us will always select others who are open, honest, and nourishing; however, with sufficient awareness of how expectations invariably damage relationships and destroy our perceptions, we become more discerning and consequently more nourishing to ourselves.

Risk-Taking

Taking risks is a powerful antidote and, for most of us, a bitter pill to swallow when we accept the fact that mutually nourishing relationships do not in themselves assure us of a resolution to our loneliness.

THE MOST EFFECTIVE RESOLUTIONS
TO LONELINESS ARE THOSE THAT
STEM FROM WITHIN OURSELVES AND
ARE A MANIFESTATION OF OUR
PERSONAL GROWTH AND DEEPENING
AWARENESS OF WHO WE ARE. THE
OUTCOME OF RISK-TAKING IS
UNPREDICTABLE BY DEFINITION.
REJECTION FORCES US, AT LEAST
MOMENTARILY, TO RELY ON OUR

INNER RESOURCES. REJECTIONS OR
OTHER KINDS OF PSYCHIC PAIN ARE
NECESSARY TO INNER GROWTH.

The resolution of loneliness and our willingness to confront ourselves with the full responsibility for it begins when we are willing to face our loneliness—or are unable to tolerate it any longer. Pain is a necessary ingredient if we are to be sufficiently motivated to risk experimenting with new attitudes and behavior *and* to tolerate the inevitable rejections. In taking risks in order to resolve our loneliness, we must recognize the value of rejection in the growth and evolution of our self and our life-style. Otherwise,

WE PERPETUATE OUR LONELINESS BY
ALLOWING OUR FEAR OF REJECTION
TO DOMINATE US.

When we are not centered, not fully motivated by our own pain and inner determination, our well-being continues to rest on chance or the responsiveness of others. This is the price we pay as long as we depend on the external world rather than our inner self for sustenance.

In our struggle to take risks, we may feel our fears and anxieties so acutely that it is difficult to believe that others may be totally unaware that anything new is emerging. People who have known us all our lives may not recognize this change. It remains our responsibility to accept how others respond, or fail to respond and, in any case, to remain centered on ourselves and what we feel we need to do to resolve our loneliness.

It is the gratification of knowing that we are breaking out of our self-imposed prison that becomes the mainstay of our continued motivation. To count primarily on the validation of others is to return to the externally oriented attitudes that generate loneliness.

In this process of evolution, it is not unusual to find that some of our existing relationships, those that in the past we may have struggled to develop or sustain, are now perceived as too destructive. We are no longer willing to continue in the same old pattern; as we evolve, our relationships also must evolve. We may find that some long-standing relationships simply become steadily less interesting.

When we have been consistently lonely, usually we have sought nourishment from people with whom we mostly experience frustration and a lack of emotional gratification. The risk-taking process usually brings new awareness of such toxic interactions and increases the likelihood that we may choose to let go of them. Our breaking out of obsolete relationships is further facilitated as we discover that there are other people who are more responsive and more nourishing. This discovery, in turn, provides a new motivation to risk more by breaking out of our own manipulative patterns, which we now see as not only poisonous but obsolete and unnecessary.

> RISK-TAKING IS A GROWTH PROCESS IN
> WHICH WE BECOME MORE AWARE OF
> THE NOURISHING AND TOXIC
> PATTERNS OF OTHERS, AND MORE
> EFFECTIVE IN RESPONDING TO THEM.

As our self-trust grows through this ongoing process of risking, we also become less vulnerable to criticism and other manipulations. These and other nourishing manifestations are the antidote process that begins as we become more aware, more centered, and more committed to taking risks.

Nourishing relating unfolds naturally when two people are genuinely open to contact with each other. This new way of relating that is so obviously more gratifying simply supersedes the long-standing patterns that generate feelings of isolation and loneliness. We just don't need those patterns any longer. For example, in crisis situations, we temporarily forget our defensiveness. Without any premeditation, we may find ourselves surrendering into the openness which such a situation demands.

> Rosemary had worked at the bank a little over two years when a dramatic event occurred:
> While I was the newest of twelve employees, I had from the beginning enjoyed the warm, friendly atmosphere. We were all friends and frequently socialized on weekends. I

didn't realize how little we really knew each other until that terrible day when four men came in brandishing guns and herded us into the vault where we spent twelve terrifying hours. We were hysterical and one man thought he was having a heart attack. The way we related to each other in this situation was different from anything I had ever known. During those long hours, sitting there waiting to be rescued, we shared in ways we had never been able to before. In those few hours, we got to know each other on a far deeper level than in the entire time I had been working there. I hope I never go through such an experience again, but I must say that ever since then our openness with each other has deepened in unbelievable ways. All of us are aware of this now and feel a deep love and caring for each other.

The idea that these people, caught up in a crisis, could be preoccupied with their usual anxiety or fear of loneliness or isolation becomes absurd. While they may have been filled with fear or intense emotions, their anxiety about rejection and loneliness disappeared.

Nourishing initiating and risk-taking follow the flow of our inner self. It is not a matter of taking ourselves by the back of the neck or dictating imperatives, but it does require effort and determination. Nourishing risk-taking is synonymous with being open and honest with ourselves about what we need, and reaching out for it as best we can. The difficulty is that we allow old fears and anxieties to paralyze us. Initiating and taking risks require action *in spite of* feelings of self-consciousness, anxiety, and apprehension.

> THE FEAR THAT DISASTER WILL OVERTAKE US IF WE REACH OUT IS A FANTASY WHICH WE CAN DISCREDIT ONLY THROUGH OUR OWN EXPERIENCE.

Analyzing and ruminating about our loneliness are frequently manifestations of our anxiety about taking risks. These mental gymnastics readily become excuses with which to avoid action.

With the best of intentions, we may believe that it is necessary to go through some sort of mental preparation in order to succeed. This attitude is self-defeating since we lose the sense of commitment to the risk-taking *process*. Instead we focus on the immediate results of each action and tend to become preoccupied with judging ourselves.

A more nourishing attitude centers on our awareness and acceptance of the fact that

> AT ANY MOMENT WE ALWAYS DO THE
> BEST WE CAN.

With this attitude, risks that lead to rejections, disappointments, or embarrassment are not mistakes, but the learning experiences without which we cannot grow.

When we are lonely, it is common to find ourselves plagued with a phobia about making "mistakes." The only way to avoid "mistakes" is to avoid taking risks or initiating anything new or different. The antidotal attitude is:

> FEEL FREE TO BE SCARED AND
> ANXIOUS ABOUT RISKING, BUT DO THE
> BEST YOU CAN ANYHOW!

We're All in the Same Boat

Many people believe their loneliness is unique, or at least uncommon, even though they frequently hear others express similar feelings. We may insist that our loneliness, our feelings of alienation and isolation are more extreme, or that our finding a resolution is somehow exceptionally difficult. This fantasy only enhances our sense of isolation.

It is important to be aware that, to one degree or another, each of us feels apprehensive and insecure about being rejected. We each have anxieties or fears about being unlovable, or other notions about why we won't be able to find what we need.

> WHEN WE FEEL OUR FEARS,
> ANXIETIES, OR "PROBLEMS" ARE
> UNIQUE, WE ARE UNDER OUR OWN
> HIGHLY TOXIC ILLUSION.

15

~~~~~~~~

Keys to Victory over Loneliness

Breaking Out of False Antidotes

The stage is set for discovering more effective antidotes to loneliness when we recognize the ineffectual antidotes we have tried in the past. False antidotes frequently have the glamour and appeal of the quick and painless remedy. They reflect our manipulations of ourselves, or others (Just listen to me! I have the answer for you if you'll just do as I say!).

False antidotes are fostered by the toxic attitude that the means are unimportant as long as we achieve the desired results. This attitude leads to patterns of behavior that, at best, provide only temporary relief or serve as psychic anesthesias. In either case, we avoid the real source of our loneliness.

Breaking Out of Paranoia

The paranoia that comes as loneliness intensifies can create within us a fear that there is a prevailing attitude of dislike or rejection emanating toward us from others. This paranoid attitude encourages us to build psychological barriers against openness and contact, since people are perceived as hostile antagonists. These feelings prejudice our perceptions even about people we have just met.

Paranoia represents a projection on others of our own hostility and frustration. We waste our energy in defending ourselves against threats which exist only in our own minds and in constantly trying to mobilize stronger defenses to protect ourselves against them. In so doing we continue to be less available for potentially nourishing relationships. Release from this paranoid attitude begins with breaking out of our external orientation which perpetuates it and focusing our awareness on becoming more self-loving and self-caring, thereby making our inner self the source of our strength and security. As this process continues, paranoia diminishes.

> AS WE LEARN TO NOURISH OURSELVES MORE EFFECTIVELY, OUR PERCEPTION OF OTHERS SHIFTS. WE ALSO BEGIN TO SEE THEM AS MORE LOVING AND NOURISHING.

We waste less energy as our paranoia diminishes. A cyclical effect develops, in which we use this energy in more nourishing ways, which lead to greater feelings of security and strength, which, in turn, lessen the power of our paranoid fantasies and our need for protective barriers.

This process is illustrated in the role-playing technique which is done in private and in seeking greater intimacy with the self. One can either talk to oneself in a mirror or imagine oneself on an empty chair.

DEBBIE:
(Talking out loud to herself, addressing an empty chair in front of her. The subject of the "dialogue" is her inner attitudes and self-concept.)

I feel there are parts of you I just haven't known. I'd like to be closer to you. I feel I know you only on a superficial basis. Suddenly, I feel sad, like I've really missed you. I also feel fearful about getting to know you. I know I run from you all the time. I don't know what scares me. I feel like: "Hey, what's wrong with you? You're okay! I might even love knowing you." I wonder why I keep running from you, why I keep putting my priorities outside myself. I want to give you more attention and importance and show I care about you. I see now how much I've been avoiding you.

The Open System

Paranoia is synonymous with a closed attitude and personality pattern that suffocate our vitality and growth. The solution to this problem involves sticking our necks out, little by little, in order to experience for ourselves, *in the present,* whether our closed-off attitude is necessary to protect ourselves or whether it is an obsolete nightmarish fantasy. Becoming more psychologically available for nourishment means breaking out of our prejudices and expectations. Yesterday's reality is not a reliable barometer of the present.

> BREAKING OUT OF PARANOIA
> INVOLVES RECOGNITION THAT
> EFFECTIVE DEFENSES AGAINST OUR
> FANTASY FEARS ARE IMPOSSIBLE.
> PARANOID DEFENSES NEVER PROVIDE
> A GENUINE FEELING OF SECURITY AND
> WELL-BEING.

With openness, the natural processes of learning how to realistically protect ourselves from whatever is destructive to our well-being will emerge. At the same time we remain open to assimilate nourishing experiences.

The ultimate goal is to become committed lifelong explorers, first, of our inner selves, and secondly, of our external world. In a state of extreme loneliness, we reverse this process and think of exploration primarily in terms of the outer world and, while this is a vital area for exploration and growth, it is of secondary importance in discovering how to live our life fully.

> IF WE ARE TO LIVE FULLY, INNER
> EXPLORATION IS ESSENTIAL. THE RISK
> OF VULNERABILITY IS A NECESSARY
> PRICE FOR EXPANSION OF OURSELVES.

The major source of growth arises from the integration of newly discovered aspects of our expanding self. There are endless explorations and infinite richness to be discovered when we turn our attention inward. The potential excitement and joy of this inner openness can become so powerful that our preoccupation with loneliness becomes increasingly meaningless.

For most of us, this inner journey is also fraught with fear and anxiety that our discoveries may be too disturbing. However, our deeper wisdom, which most of us are unaware of and few of us trust, will prevail and protect us if we do not *try* to probe into ourselves, or to *dig* for new discoveries. To begin we need only to pay attention to what *is*. We allow our inner self to emerge and we focus our attention on this awareness process. This is the emergence of the self in its natural step-by-step growth.

> GROWTH OF THE SELF OCCURS
> SPONTANEOUSLY WHEN WE STOP
> HAMPERING THIS NATURAL PROCESS.

This may mean taking the risk of experimenting with breaking out of our lifelong closed attitudes and allowing our openness to unfold. Try as we might, we cannot reassure ourselves ahead of time that what awaits us is the discovery of our paranoia.

Simplifying

When we are willing to risk opening ourselves, both inwardly and with others, there is an enormous enhancement of our ability to discriminate between what is nourishing and what is toxic. We discover the simplicity of reality and become able to channel our energies toward more effective responsiveness to the ever-present sources of nourishment. Similarly, we begin to reclaim our wasted energies as we lessen our involvement in what we now see is the enormous amount of unnecessary trivia that we have allowed to clutter our lives. A nourishing chain reaction evolves, in which our openness leads to greater discrimination, which, in turn, leads to greater simplification.

Randee loved her challenging, creative job in a large advertising agency. She was twenty-seven and was already earning $30,000 a year, plus bonuses. Yet, out of habit, she persisted in spending two evenings a week doing laundry and other chores she thoroughly disliked. In order to save a few dollars a month, she would shop at a market three miles away, rather than at a more convenient store. She lived in her own condominium and did all the minor repairs, even though this maintenance, too, was drudgery. She hated doing dishes, yet would not buy a dishwasher. In many other ways, Randee wasted her time and energy on menial chores that were totally ungratifying.

She clung to friends she had long outgrown and whom she found dull and boring; yet she often refused invitations to meet new people because her time was so consumed with trivia and obsolete relationships. In other areas of her life, her anxieties and insecurities also dictated her choices. She had a strong interest in art and history, but her friends pressured her to focus on current events and political issues in order to be more interesting.

Despite her successful and busy life, Randee was a lonely person. Her complicated life, filled with busywork, was her way of avoiding confronting herself about her real needs. She knew she wanted to experiment, meet new people, do different things, and be more responsive to her inner needs, yet she avoided this and continued to live according to what others expected of her.

Randee lived dominated by the common fear that being her own self and responding to her experiences by eliminating what was not meaningful or gratifying would lead to loneliness and isolation.

Like Randee, the lonely often fill their lives with busywork that only wastes time and energy. Similarly, when we allow our attitudes and behavior to be dictated by other people, we complicate our existence enormously by dissipating ourselves.

Cluttering our lives with trivial activities easily becomes

an automatic, self-perpetuating pattern, performed in a ritualistic manner without considering the necessity of it or the lack of personal gratification. We may be unaware how each insignificant aspect of this trivia adds up to a constant drain on our time and energy. It is easy to rationalize this because each separate instance is so insignificant; yet, when added together over a period of time, they are enormous in their poisonous draining effect on our vitality.

A Simplified Approach to Rejection

Loneliness may lead to such a preoccupation with rejection, and the fear of it, that it becomes the center of our lives. Our relationships, interests, and activities, even our choice of occupation, may largely be dictated by our need to avoid rejection no matter what the cost. In relating to others, our concern may primarily be focused on how secure a relationship seems to be, a criterion which takes priority over nourishment.

> WHILE IT IS PAINFUL TO BE REJECTED,
> ESPECIALLY WHEN WE ARE INTENSELY
> INVOLVED EMOTIONALLY, MOST OF
> THE PAIN IS DUE TO OUR PERSONAL
> ATTITUDES.

For example, we may see rejection as a bad reflection on our self-esteem or as an affront to our ego. This attitude about rejection may be more painful than the actual loss of someone with whom we have been involved.

The no-risk attitude we may adopt in our struggle to avoid loneliness is often expressed by our reluctance to commit ourselves to relationships we really know are meaningful and gratifying, because of our fear of rejection. For example, some people are tremendously open and affectionate with animals and small children, while this loving responsiveness is lacking in their relations to other adults for whom they have similar feelings.

Rejection is painful, but rarely does it hurt as much or as long as our fantasy suggests. In any case, when we wait for our fear of rejection to go away, we are apt to wait forever. The fear of rejection, for most of us, doesn't clear up. Instead the simple (but not easy) antidote is:

IT'S OKAY TO BE AFRAID OF REJECTION
AS LONG AS OUR FEAR DOESN'T
PREVENT US FROM REACHING OUT
FOR WHAT WE WANT.

Some anxiety about intimate relationships is unavoidable. Guarantees against rejection are not possible, regardless of good intentions and promises, including marital vows.

When we are lonely and too fearful of rejection, we may try to avoid our own awareness of the deterioration of a relationship. Our agony is only intensified by this avoidance.

Rejection commonly occurs when an initially nourishing relationship begins to become increasingly meaningless because the other person has gradually become less interested. To avoid this rejection, we may manipulate ourselves or the other person by trying to sustain a relationship when we already know it is no longer nourishing. Out of fear that rejection is intolerable, we create more frustration and loneliness and, in the long run, we end up having to face the inevitable rejection.

When we become aware of a relationship in which the emotional nourishment is diminishing, it is best to confront ourselves and our partner with our feelings. Both separately and together, we can consider possible remedies. Pursuing these possibilities is a nourishing endeavor, regardless of the outcome. It provides us with the opportunity to explore fully whether or not we feel there is a reasonable prospect of resolving our difficulties and continuing our relationship.

A RELATIONSHIP IN WHICH WE NO
LONGER FEEL LOVED AND NOURISHED
IS TANTAMOUNT TO REJECTION.

Open confrontation helps avoid unnecessary frustration and loneliness. When it does not lead to a resolution, it at least provides us with the knowledge that we have done the best we can to maintain the relationship and ease the pain of letting go.

A mourning process is inevitable when someone we love decides the relationship is over. We are then the rejected one. We are cut off from what has been a source of emotional nourishment.

> BREAKING OUT OF AN INTIMATE RELATIONSHIP THAT HAS BECOME INCREASINGLY DESTRUCTIVE IS AN EFFECTIVE ANTIDOTE FOR THE RESOLUTION AND/OR AVOIDANCE OF LONELINESS. THE EMOTIONAL BREAKING OUT, THE MOURNING OF OUR LOSS MUST BE COMPLETED IF WE ARE TO BECOME FULLY AVAILABLE FOR NEW RELATIONSHIPS.

An Exercise in Breaking Out of Rejection

Imagine yourself breaking out of a rejecting relationship by saying good-bye to it, as you shake your hands with the fingers hanging loosely. At the same time blow air out through your mouth; imagine you are eliminating letting go of your attachments to the person rejecting you by shaking them out of your mind and body. Then look around and become aware of what nourishment *is* available.

Toxic relationships, as well as destructive thoughts and behavior, don't die easily; they keep popping up to plague us. This exercise can be used as needed. The optimal attitude is to be without condemnation, judgment, or annoyance with yourself when these thoughts and feelings of being rejected continue to recur. Simply realize that you are still holding on with your mind (and therefore with your body) to that which is now obsolete.

It is madness to believe we can somehow manipulate ourselves or others into sustaining a nourishing relationship when we are being rejected.

> ONE-WAY RELATIONSHIPS ARE ALWAYS SELF-DEFEATING.

The process of breaking out when we have been rejected involves facing and accepting our anger, resentment, and other hostilities. When we cling to our anger toward another person who has rejected us, or whom we have rejected, we continue to poison ourselves.

When we feel rejected, any pattern of self-blame, self-criticism, or guilt is a manifestation of anger turned inward. It is another way of holding on to the past and has no value whatsoever. Furthermore, to the extent that we feel like a failure or feel unworthy or unlovable, we hold ourselves emotionally unavailable for new relationships.

The Best Way Out Is Through

When we have been chronically lonely for long periods of time, usually we have spent much of our energy avoiding the pain of our loneliness rather than seeking to discover effective pathways from it. Avoiding the pain of loneliness makes it increasingly ominous and fearsome. We thereby allow our loneliness to become bigger than ourselves. And the more fearsome we make it, the faster we have to run. All the toxic games discussed previously exemplify the numerous ways in which each of us runs our own kind of rat race. This may continue endlessly as long as we avoid going through the pain of facing up to our loneliness and in that way begin to break out of it. At times we may sincerely believe that our avoidance and other manipulations of ourselves are not only helpful but the best we can do to cope with the pain of our loneliness.

> WHEN WE REFUSE TO ACKNOWLEDGE
> FULLY THAT WE ARE LONELY, WE
> HANDICAP OURSELVES IN SEEKING AN
> EFFECTIVE RESOLUTION.

We rarely allow ourselves the fullest experience of our loneliness; we rarely accept the fact that our loneliness is part of our experiential self.

Our examination of loneliness can generate the motivation

and determination to break out of it and makes the likelihood of an effective resolution optimal.

THE PAIN AND FEAR OF LONELINESS DIMINISH THE MORE FULLY WE ALLOW OURSELVES TO EXPERIENCE IT.

The human mind has a tremendous ability to create such intense reactions within us that it may be difficult to accept the fact that these are our own concoctions. The *fear* of loneliness is usually more devastating than loneliness itself. Similarly, thoughts and fantasies of future loneliness are frequently more painful and more destructive than actual loneliness.

Going into (and therefore eventually through) our loneliness as often as necessary is a way of making friends with a part of ourselves that we have in the past disowned. When we are willing to risk giving up our futile attempts to isolate ourselves from our loneliness, the integration that follows frees the energy previously trapped in maintaining this self-fragmenting process and enables us to mobilize our resources far more effectively than is otherwise possible.

GOING THROUGH OUR LONELINESS IS THE BEST WAY TO BREAK OUT OF IT!

This is analogous to coping with physical pain. The more we tense up, the more we attempt to brace ourselves against physical pain, the more pain we actually create. In contrast, when we are willing to accept the pain and relax, it becomes less intense. When we surrender into our lonely feelings our pain will gradually lessen and the energy we have freed (now that we no longer need to fight *against* our loneliness) is available to discover more effective resolutions.

This requires a shift in attitude in which our loneliness is accepted as a normal human emotion which all of us experience. We discover that we can diminish its power by ceasing to struggle against it as if it were an alien force rather than an aspect of ourselves.

An Exercise in Integrating All
of One's Self

Seat yourself in a chair with another chair directly in front of you. Now, imagine that in another chair you are sitting as you were when you were a child of four, six, or eight years of age. Talk to that little child. Try using words such as "big" and "little" to represent adult and childish aspects of the self. Imagine the child to be frightened, insecure, and lonely. Imagine that he or she needs the support and strength of the adult in you to cope with your loneliness. Talk to your "child" with the awareness that this little person is still a part of you. Be aware of any criticism, embarrassment, or avoidance of your childlike self. For example, John, a thirty-six-year-old man, had the following dialogue with himself after getting over the initial embarrassment, using this technique for the first time.

BIG JOHN: I wish you'd grow up. Why can't you be like me? I don't let things bother me. I'm strong and I don't like seeing so many weaknesses in you.

LITTLE JOHN: I'm not weak. I'm just little. I can't help it if I feel scared. We live in the same body. Why can't you take care of me? Let me be who I am without always putting me down!

BIG JOHN: I never looked at you that way. But you must admit that you're a lot of trouble—always getting scared, feeling lonely, or unloved.

LITTLE JOHN: I also play, have fun, and bring excitement into our life. All you do is worry about responsibilities and appearances. Yes, I'm scared many times. It would help if you'd reassure me, tell me you love me, instead of acting so ashamed of me. Without me, you wouldn't be very human—you'd be more like an unfeeling machine. Now, please tell me you love me.

BIG JOHN: I . . . I . . . I don't know why this is so hard to do. I . . . love you, Little John, just as you are.

LITTLE JOHN: Thank you, Big John. I need that more

than anything. And I love you, too. I don't think I'm going to feel so lonely anymore!

Available Others

HOW IS IT POSSIBLE TO BE LONELY WHEN ALL AROUND US ARE COUNTLESS OTHER PEOPLE?

Loneliness blinds us to reality. We act as if the world around us were one big clique, in which everyone fits but us.

In seeking new intimacies, it is important for us to be aware of people who, for reasons of their own, are not interested and therefore not available.

Developing intimate relationships does not come simply by sharing time, interests, or activities; intimacy does not follow any schedule or effort. Limited responsiveness that does not deepen usually suggests that the highest degree of potential intimacy has been reached. We can either accept limited intimacy or recognize it and move on. Especially when we have been lonely, we may believe we can or should be able to deepen the relationship single-handedly. Even more dangerous, we may try to analyze the reasons for our "failure." A more nourishing attitude, when we are aware that our desire to relate more intimately is not reciprocated, is to break out and move on, knowing that the world is full of "available others" looking for intimacy.

PEOPLE SEEKING INTIMATE RELATIONSHIPS WILL NEVER BE IN SHORT SUPPLY. UNFORTUNATELY, WHEN WE ARE CHRONICALLY LONELY, THIS IS OFTEN THE MOST DIFFICULT TRUTH TO BELIEVE.

The Nourishment of Pain

Intense loneliness is always reflected in some form of physical distress which is a clear message that a state of emotional deprivation exists. While it is unusual for us to conceive of emotional pain as valuable, the pain of loneliness speaks with a purpose. As its intensity increases, it expresses a growing urgency that demands a response.

Our recognition of these disturbing body messages allows us to respond to them in a nourishing fashion. When we are willing to look, we usually find considerable insight into our avoidance of confrontation. Most of us, for example, are aware of the catastrophes we anticipate when we realize that (thus far) loneliness has been a major preoccupation in our lives. Avoidance only perpetuates our stalemate and invites more loneliness. Avoiding our pain remains easier than risking doing something effective to resolve it.

When we have the courage to give up our games and manipulations, we're ready to listen to what our deeper self is saying. The pain of our loneliness is then recognized as valuable. This, in itself, facilitates the search for a resolution. New possibilities of action emerge and new energy, previously trapped in our endless deadlock of avoiding loneliness, is freed and can now be used more effectively and creatively.

A shift in attitudes may change our entire perception of the world. Loneliness is subjective; it is personal and arbitrary. For example, when someone else is present, for instance a child asleep in another room, we may spend many enjoyable hours involved in solitary activity. Knowing there is another person in the house, even though there is no interaction, often alleviates loneliness. Under the same circumstances, but with no one at home, our attitude may shift into deep loneliness. What was experienced as enjoyable and nourishing becomes largely a distraction to avoid the pain of loneliness.

WHEN WE DISCOVER HOW ARBITRARY
OUR ATTITUDE IS ABOUT LONELINESS,
INFINITE NEW POSSIBILITIES FOR ITS
RESOLUTION EMERGE.

Anger and Loneliness

All of us get angry. While it is healthier to express our anger than constantly to suppress it, it is also true that anger alienates others. Anger may be a way of breaking through the barriers that have been created between people and have hampered their ability to relate more intimately. The expression of anger becomes a gateway to more nourishing relationships. Nevertheless, the expression of anger when it serves to break the isolation or to bring about a confrontation in order to resolve differences that are destructive to a relationship is, at best, only a step in relating intimately. Typically, chronically lonely people settle for the relief of having "gotten it out!" Such catharsis is superficial and endless and fosters an attitude in which intimates increasingly relate to each other as antagonists.

> WHEN WE ARE CHRONICALLY LONELY,
> WE ARE FREQUENTLY CHRONICALLY
> ANGRY ALSO.

The popular idea that the expression of anger is "good" is nonsense. Expression of anger splits intimate partners into two warring camps, each trying to gain some advantage over the other.

> ANGER IS A MANIFESTATION OF OUR
> OWN UNFULFILLED EXPECTATIONS
> WHICH WE PROJECT ONTO ANOTHER
> PERSON.

Anger reflects the angry person's own arbitrary opinion of how others *should* respond, or relate, even how others *should* think and feel.

> WHEN, IN SEEKING RESOLUTIONS TO
> OUR LONELINESS, WE ARE WILLING TO
> ACCEPT THE REALITY THAT, IN
> INTIMATE RELATING, NO ONE IS
> SUPPOSED TO BE DIFFERENT FROM
> HOW THEY ARE, THE WAY IS OPEN FOR
> A NEW ATTITUDE IN RELATING
> TO OTHERS WITHOUT ANGER.

We must recognize that underneath our anger is always our criticism of others. ("If you would just listen to me, I wouldn't be angry at you!")

This attitude is the unconditional acceptance of others *as they are* but does not mean we like everything about them. It means breaking out of the games of manipulation and trying to change others. This is true even when we sincerely believe that our efforts are for their own good, or that our criticisms or expectations are not only reasonable but in their best interests.

The nourishing attitude about the frictions and disagreements which invariably occur in all relationships is manifested when we are willing to accept responsibility for all our resentments and the way in which we express them. A relationship that lacks resentment or anger is unreal. It is one in which frictions are suppressed, as if they will then disappear. This well-meant attitude may be effective temporarily. However, energy that is locked into suppressed resentments continues to build and will burst forth with far greater force and violence.

The difference between the nourishing and true expression of anger and resentment may become clear when we understand the difference between speaking in the first person and speaking in the second person. The word "I" is more clearly an expression of the self, in which we take responsibility for our anger; in contrast, "you" is usually expressed with a finger-pointing attitude, implying that the other person is wrong and should change.

> TOM: You make me angry when you're late. You ought to be more considerate. You should make it a point to get ready early, even if you have to wait for me, rather than be late.

The same resentment expressed in a nourishing way is illustrated in the following:

> NAN: I resent your lateness. I resent constantly having to wait for you.

In a nourishing approach to anger we also take responsibility for what we are going to do when the other person remains the same. For example, Nan might decide that she will schedule herself as if the meeting time is a half hour later than she agreed. She might decide to accept that her friend is chronically late and let it go at that. Or, if her annoyance is intense, she might choose to let go of the relationship.

There are many nourishing resolutions to resentments. They all involve taking responsibility for ourselves but do not require the cooperation of the other person.

In breaking out of our anger to resolve our loneliness, it is important to keep these basic concepts in mind:

1. Each of us has a point beyond which our anger will burst forth either at others or against ourselves.
2. Angry outbursts usually bring an immediate sense of relief.
3. Feeling and expressing anger is natural and inevitable.
4. Constant expressions of anger are self-destructive.

For example, two people who are intimately involved may have a "good fight," ventilate their anger, and feel better. The fact remains that while they are angry they are combative antagonists. Usually, in an intimate relationship, one person is more capable of expressing anger or accepting it than the other. Inevitably, this means the other person takes more of a psychological beating.

ANGER ONLY BREEDS MORE ANGER.

The "loser" may yield, for the moment, and submit or retreat from the onslaught of the "winner." Sooner or later, consciously or not, the loser's anger will re-emerge. In this way a dangerous cycle of continuing hostility develops. While we cannot simply control our emotions as if we were pressing a button to turn off our anger, it is important to be aware that anger, with few exceptions, is toxic.

The acceptance of this attitude offers an antidote that is appropriate to a majority of intimate relations. When we recognize that anger, in the long run, creates a state of alienation, isolation, and loneliness, this awareness can direct us toward breaking out of it.

ANGER IS INVARIABLY AN EXPRESSION
OF AN UNDERLYING ATTITUDE THAT
THE OTHER PERSON HAS NOT MET OUR
EXPECTATIONS. WHEN OUR ANGER IS
IMPLODED AGAINST THE SELF, IT IS A
MANIFESTATION OF OUR FAILURE TO
LIVE UP TO OUR IDEALIZED SELF-IMAGE.

The insistence that, if our intimates behaved differently, these angry outbursts would not occur, is tantamount to expecting the other person to be like ourselves.

Chronically lonely people are often not only chronically angry but usually justify their anger in a self-righteous manner, citing specific occasions and acts reflecting the abuses of others (all or most of which may be true). In contrast, when we are willing to look at our own anger with even a moderate degree of open-mindedness, the esssential statement is: "Be like me. Think as I think. Feel as I feel and want what I want, and I won't get angry at you."

Being Loving

One of the most positive characteristics of nourishing people is their ability to radiate a warm, loving energy toward others. This is a natural, spontaneous style that is inherent in all of us. It is not an attitude that requires work or effort to be manifested. While all of us have this potential, the more nourishing we are, the more these feelings are reflected in our attitudes and behavior, both inwardly and outwardly. When we are being loving, it causes a positive vibration that naturally attracts others and creates an excitement that energizes them in the same way.

BEING LOVING IS THE SINGLE MOST
POWERFUL ANTIDOTE TO LONELINESS.

When we are caught up in the deprivation of intense loneliness, we have almost always lost our ability to be loving. Instead, when we are chronically lonely, we radiate a kind of negative energy toward others. Whether we are aware of it or not, we tend to draw psychological energy from others. We are primarily focused on being loved rather than being loving. Others sense this, realize that intimate contact will drain their energy, and adopt self-protective patterns. We often wonder, when we are lonely, why it is that our attempts to develop new relationships seem to fail continuously. It is our attitude, *how* we relate, that is the crucial point.

Each of us has a loving center which we can open to express these loving, radiant feelings. Many chronically lonely people have never experienced their own lovingness, their own capacity to give without expectations. Since they feel so deprived and empty of love, a focus on being loving rather than being loved may be the last thing they would consider as an antidote to their loneliness.

This attitude of being loving, radiating a feeling of love to others, does not necessarily mean doing anything in particular. It is a way of viewing ourselves and our world that can fill us with a sense of self-love instead of loneliness. Discovering how to relate to ourselves in a loving fashion involves giving up all well-meant endeavors to earn love or to prove to ourselves or others that we deserve love. This includes letting go of efforts to exonerate ourselves or atone for past deeds or feelings of guilt and shame.

> ALL ATTEMPTS TO QUALIFY AS
> "LOVABLE" ARE TOXIC.

As always, the best we can do about the past, whatever our regrets, is to break out of it and begin *now* to be the person we want to be.

Compassion

Compassion is an attitude of loving acceptance toward others in which we share their feelings in a nonjudgmental fashion. Compassion toward ourselves *as we are*, including what we don't like or may wish to change, is a manifestation of self-love. When we are compassionate toward ourselves, we are then also compassionate toward others *as they are*. This includes those with whom we seek intimacy as well as those we may have been intimate with and now wish to reject. In the latter instance, letting go with compassion and forgiveness means letting go of our hurts and our anger as well as all our blaming games.

Compassion is an energy-freeing experience that fills us with joy and excitement and radiates an attitude of "unconditional love." It is a powerful antidote against clinging to old angers and resentments with which, like dead weight, we sometimes continue to burden ourselves for many years. Often we are unaware of this "unfinished business" until we break out of our emotional stalemate and experience for ourselves the power of the release of energy and its accompanying positive resurgence of openness to the here and now.

Exercise in Compassion

Using the empty-chair method, talk to yourself compassionately, without criticism, demands, judgments, evaluations, or comparisons. Totally accept yourself and recognize the fact that, in the past, you always did the best you could at the time, regardless of your subsequent remorse or present hindsight ("If only I had . . ."). This kind of dialogue is not intended as a way of excusing yourself. It is simply a breaking away from obsolete attitudes. Compassion is a way of being more fully open to the unfolding present.

In a similar exercise, look into a mirror and say *out loud:* "I love you." Repeat this ten or fifteen times while maintaining eye contact. For most people, the initial embarrassment about this technique is considerable. This is a reflection of a lack of compassion and inner intimacy within ourselves. If it is difficult to do this, ask yourself why. Look directly into the mirror and realize that you are not perfect but are capable of loving and being loved. If *you* realize that by saying "I love you," to yourself and gradually, if not immediately, accept this truth, you embark on the path away from self-induced loneliness.

As we become more compassionate, each of us can ask our selves, "Is what I am doing now being loving?"

Our way of relating, giving, and sharing then has a different quality from the way we relate when we feel deeply lonely. We are less conscious of ourselves as "givers." Rather, compassion makes our giving a spontaneous act that we are not interested in evaluating. It is a sharing of ourselves in which we feel connected to another person in a way that is gratifying and fulfilling in itself.

Humor and Laughter

Any kind of lightheartedness is difficult when we are chronically lonely. We may feel that we have lost our sense of humor or, more commonly, that we are so unhappy that humor or laughter is inappropriate. While we never really lose any of our qualities, in loneliness our ability to see the lighter side of life seems to have died, leaving us with only our suffering.

Many of us, when deeply lonely, look as if we have been ravaged by a terrible disease. There is a mask of loneliness, as if our faces have been frozen in an expression reflecting our constant pain and depression. To add to our pain, it is not unusual to behave as if humor and levity are taboo. Only at times can a suppressed smile or incipient laughter be seen. Consciously or not, this can evolve into a toxic game in which we quietly squelch any humorous reaction, as if we would be embarrassed to break out of our loneliness and enjoy some laughter, even for a moment. We may even feel that an expression of joy might alleviate the concern of others who care about us and are struggling to find some answer for us.

Humor can be an antidote to loneliness when we let go of the fantasy that some complex, intricate process must be discovered before we can even hope for a resolution or that our struggle against loneliness necessitates the full mobilization of all our resources, as if we must commit ourselves to total war.

Like many antidotes, humor offers a simple remedy, but one that is not necessarily easy. While there are, of course, serious aspects to breaking out of our loneliness, seeing ourselves and the whole of our life as a relentless struggle against pain and suffering reflects our loss of contact with reality. Real laughter is a spontaneous happening that can take over our entire self and can literally breathe life into our bodies.

When, for example, we "roar with laughter," we shake ourselves loose from our morbid preoccupations and, at least for the moment, come to our senses. Real laughter cannot be contrived, it simply emerges and runs its course. Any such experience opens us to an examination of those attitudes and behavior patterns that make us depressed and lonely. Laughter is a shift in attitude which puts us in touch with the reality that, despite our pain and anguish, there *is* great joy in simply being alive. Spontaneous laughter is a natural and very potent antidote to the various tensions that arise in any relationship. It melts away anxieties, frustrations, and resentments. In our intimate relationships, the joy of laughter is a prime source of emotional nourishment.

LAUGHTER *IS* AN ANTIDOTE TO
LONELINESS.

Our goal, then, is to allow our humor to emerge, to become aware how often we suppress our life-giving joyousness.

It is not unusual, when we are around someone who is feeling lonely, to refrain from any levity or humor, as if laughter would be disrespectful or insensitive. We may act as if we were in the presence of someone in deep mourning. Indeed, when we feel lonely, our own laughter, to say nothing of that of others, may seem inappropriate, as if it is an obsolete remnant from happier times in the past. We have simply cut off a source of nourishment.

When we are willing to surrender to humor, to experience laughter, we discover that we are not locked in the grip of our loneliness as hopelessly as we might have imagined. Whenever we are able to break out of any painful emotional state, even for an instant, it means that the potential exists for more such experiences. Our ability to break out remains unlimited.

16

Get What You Want

Allowing

Regardless of our patterns of self-induced loneliness, potential nourishment is always available. When we are lonely, knowingly or not, we continue to isolate ourselves from this nourishment, even though we may be suffering intense emotional deprivation. Out of fear, anxiety, or insecurity, we have closed down and we refuse to risk opening ourselves, since this means exposing our vulnerability.

"Allowing" is an attitude in which we simply open ourselves to the endless possibilities that are available. Antidotal "allowing" begins when we risk letting down our defenses and becoming more receptive to the initiating actions of others. It is a kind of open passivity that provides a balance to our own self-initiating activities.

> WHEN WE ARE LONELY WE DO NOT
> ALWAYS HAVE TO ASSERT OURSELVES.
> AT TIMES ALL THAT IS REQUIRED IS
> TO BE OPEN AND RECEPTIVE TO THE
> NOURISHMENT THAT IS BEING OFFERED
> TO US.

Nourishing experiences happen all the time without our initiating them. One need only be in the sunlight to experience its warmth. Sitting quietly and doing nothing is often a nourishing posture that radiates a feeling of openness and availability to others. This can be a very attractive mood, which encourages others to reach out to us. "Allowing" involves the risk of breaking out of our self-imposed pressure to do something constantly, to try harder, or to pursue more activities.

Safety in Numbers

It is in the quality, not the quantity, of relationships that effective interpersonal resolutions to loneliness are to be found. When we are lonely, we may assume that we just can't have too many friends. Because of our anxiety of future loneliness, and in spite of a wide circle of friends, we may blindly continue our quest for more and more relationships. Without realizing it, we may spread ourselves so thin emotionally that the potential for intimacy is diminished simply by the limits on our available time and energy.

> NONE OF US CAN RELATE IN A DEEPLY
> INTIMATE, ONGOING FASHION TO MORE
> THAN A HANDFUL OF PEOPLE AT ANY
> ONE TIME. NOR DO WE NEED TO!

In the "more is better" kind of relating, the principal preoccupation is to avoid losing touch with others rather than to look for deeper, more meaningful, ongoing relationships. This attitude also ignores the need of others for intimacy and depth. Nourishing people are likely to be frustrated or disinterested when we are so busy that we are only available infrequently or superficially; they will then seek out more responsive people.

A "safety in numbers" attitude inevitably generates superficial relationships. It is essential that we become more aware of the difference between acquaintances and intimate relationships. The greater our need for intimacy, the more we need to seek a relatively small number of sustained relationships. While this may create considerable anxiety when we are trying to insure ourselves against loneliness, the alternative, always having lots of people around, aborts deeper intimacy.

Many lonely people fantasize that they must always have

someone available. Greater intimacy with oneself is a necessary aspect in the antidote to this pattern. Inevitably, there will be times when we *are* alone and have no choice, and we then need to learn how to accept, and enjoy, our solitude.

The Cycle of Trust

THE GREATEST OBSTACLE TO BREAKING OUT OF LONELINESS IS A LACK OF *SELF-TRUST.*

Most of us, in both obvious and subtle ways, have been taught not to trust our inner self. Parents and the culture instill in us the fear, if not the belief, that we are inadequate, unworthy, and unlovable. Perhaps many of us still believe that without the controlling power of guilt, shame, and fear we could not live together in a civilized manner. This is a manifestation of the essential lack of self-trust that dominates our culture.

Each of us naturally grows into a healthy, nourishing person if not taught, particularly during the vulnerable years of childhood, to distrust ourselves. Similarly, in adulthood, if we decide to stop torturing ourselves with improvement programs and other well-intended resolutions and learn to be self-trusting and self-loving *as we are,* we will evolve naturally into loving, caring people.

In contrast, the chronically lonely adopt the toxic attitudes learned in the past and continue to criticize themselves in much the same way that they were victimized by well-meaning adults during their childhood. Self-trust involves taking the risk of breaking out of such obsolete, self-poisoning patterns. In this way, we open ourselves and feel more loving, accepting and trusting of ourselves.

To let ourselves be, to allow ourselves to accept every inner thought or feeling, to break out of our criticalness, fears, and anxieties, and trust our deeper wisdom, means less torment and more growth and nourishment. Then we discover our inner self-determining powers and, more importantly, our ability to love and be loved.

SELF-TRUST IS BASIC FOR GROWTH AND
FOR THE ULTIMATE RESOLUTION OF
LONELINESS.

When our feelings of self-trust begin to emerge naturally, the destructive, traumatic experiences from our past correspondingly fade into the background. The memories of these traumas may linger, but their toxic power is gone. For most of us, nurturing self-trust is risky. Fear and anxiety are, to some degree, to be expected. We must be willing to risk trusting our feelings, needs, and decisions—and actively responding to them *in spite of* our fears and anxieties. As our self-trust grows, it, in turn, generates another nourishing cycle of expanding openness in relating inwardly and to others, and our feelings of loneliness and isolation recede.

Regardless of past hurts, whether from childhood or more recent, the present cycle of new, more nourishing experiences simply supersedes the old, since the new experiences are more gratifying. Integration of new experiences helps us to break out of our loneliness-inducing patterns, which will flourish only as long as our old distrust of ourselves, with its closed-off, isolating effect, is allowed to persist. The cycle of trust, once established, continues to grow, and with it grows our attitude of trust toward other people. A new and different mental attitude emerges, which encourages positive intimacy and, in this way, a resolution to loneliness.

Tell Me What to Do

Seeking out or following the "helpful" suggestions offered by well-meaning people is a way of perpetuating our loneliness. When we complain about our anguish and express our desperation, it is often a subtle way of drawing others into the futile role of trying to provide us with the right answer.

Regardless of the good faith with which suggestions are offered, these "why don't you . . ." kinds of advice only deepen our loneliness and isolation in the long run. Such suggestions are usually discarded or met with excuses, showing lack of the inner determination necessary to make a commitment to follow the suggestion.

The antidote for this dead-end approach—that someone else has the answer—involves breaking out of this externally oriented attitude and facing the reality (initially quite an unpleasant one) that our power to break out of loneliness must emerge from within.

> THE EFFECTIVE RESOLUTION TO
> LONELINESS IS AN INNER-ORIENTED
> PROCESS THAT MUST BE INITIATED
> AND SUSTAINED FROM WITHIN.

This attitude is necessary in order to learn how to develop our inner potentials. Only when we experience these inner discoveries can we accept fully that they do, in fact, exist. We *must* discover these hidden resources for ourselves in order to believe their power.

> WHEN WE HAVE BEEN DEEPLY LONELY,
> WE TEND TO HOPE AND EVEN TO
> EXPECT THAT THE RIGHT
> RELATIONSHIP, OR THE RIGHT PATTERN
> OF ACTIVITIES, WILL RESOLVE OUR
> LONELINESS.

The subtle trap inherent in these expectations is that many such experiences do indeed result in an alleviation of our loneliness. However, when our excitement is largely based on the stimulation of something new, it usually dwindles and, in the long run, only becomes another detour. The inner patterns causing our self-induced loneliness have only been short-circuited for a while.

In contrast, turning inward and facing our emptiness, lack of self-trust, and fear of failure, while it is a more painful process, presents real possibilities for substantial creative resolutions. Only then will we know that effective resolutions have always been within our untapped potentials.

Patience

Patience is an expression of self-love and self-trust, and is essential if we are to stay centered. It is a nonjudgmental attitude that disregards our well-intended schedules, comparisons, and self-improvement campaigns, which are as meaningless in the long run as a "miraculous ten-day diet." When, in contrast, we are impatient, we poison ourselves with judgments and expectations. Patience means allowing the spontaneous flow of the self to emerge as a natural process of our inner motivations. A state of readiness to act, a willingness to respond to our inner needs then emerges. We stop pushing and manipulating ourselves. The timing of our risk-taking actions reflects the fact that we are directed from our own center.

Our push-button society teaches us impatience. We are taught to expect quick, easy, and painless results. When we are impatient we are not fully behind our own actions and are prone to act impulsively.

In seeking antidotes to loneliness, our achievement-oriented, do-it-now cultural attitudes demand enough force to overcome whatever resistance may appear. Looking for a quick solution to loneliness fosters our impatience. It is an attempt to avoid the reality that breaking out of loneliness is a process—not a sudden act.

Similarly, when we are lonely, we may think we have no control over our lives and must either remain at the mercy of others or face even more intense feelings of alienation and abandonment. We then constrain ourselves, while hoping that an outstanding achievement, for example, will provide some kind of reaction from others that will resolve our loneliness. Since, of course, this never happens, our frustration grows, our tolerance diminishes, and we feel more impatient.

Impatience is also enhanced by keeping records of our performance. Comparisons, whether favorable or not, are negative. Evaluating our progress interferes with our ability to function as fully as possible in the moment. It may, for example, be difficult not to become impatient when we continue to avoid taking risks because of old fears and anxieties. Any self-effacing comments, even when said silently to ourselves, only increase our impatience and make our risk-taking ventures even more difficult.

Usually we are taught that more is better and having everything right now is best of all. The illusion that we should be able to find easy solutions to our loneliness further drains our ability to be lovingly patient with ourselves, to live fully, and to stay centered on the process of discovering our inner self, regardless of how we decide to grade our progress. The more demanding our arbitrary grading system, the more we tax our patience unnecessarily. When impatience takes over, we may react impulsively, indulging in various activities that provide some immediate temporary relief or gratification; for example, eating or drinking binges or sexual promiscuity. The usual rationalization is that this will somehow renew our patience and motivation. In reality, these indulgences only lead to more of the frustrating, ungratifying attitudes and behavior that have habitually hampered our ability to be patient with ourselves. It is vital to persist on the path we know is, at the time, the best one to resolve our loneliness.

Trying Versus Wanting

In the face of difficulties, our usual attitude is that we should simply try harder in our efforts involving our relations with ourselves, our inner growth, and our resolution of our loneliness. Trying is a manipulation of the self that encourages an inner split; part of the self asserts its power in an attempt to overwhelm another part. This is analogous to accelerating an automobile while the brakes are on. This kind of effort tends to burn out our motivation even when we produce results. Trying fosters within us the illusion that life is a continuous ordeal, that any action demands an enormous amount of energy.

In contrast, when we are self-nourishing, the self-manipulative, forced approach characteristic of trying is minimal. Our efforts are more in keeping with our natural flow of needs. We don't push ourselves excessively and, instead, wait while our inner motivation becomes more compelling, until we feel a genuine desire that generates its own motivation. With this attitude, the amount of energy we waste coping with inner conflicts is minimal.

Generally, in applying antidotes to loneliness, the more intense our motivation to overcome our toxic patterns, the greater the likelihood the antidotes will be effective. In contrast, when we are not sufficiently motivated to want to change, our energy is largely channeled toward manipulating ourselves into "trying."

When we feel lonely, we may resolve, in good faith, to "try" to break our self-destructive patterns or initiate new, more nourishing ones. Since the power of the self is divided against itself, these efforts are usually short-lived bursts of enthusiasm followed by frustration, despair, and deeper resignation.

THERE IS A NATURAL TIMING TO OUR BREAKING OUT OF LONELINESS THAT DEVELOPS WITHIN US AND CANNOT BE PROGRAMMED. OUR READINESS FOR CHANGE EMERGES FROM WITHIN WHEN WE HAVE *REALLY* HAD ENOUGH.

When we pay attention to our deeper feelings, we know when we are ready to begin risking and experimenting. When we move prematurely, an unnecessarily tedious effort follows, which usually turns out to be another frustrating exercise in futility. When we become aware that trying is self-manipulative and begin to trust our inner self to mobilize us into readiness, our efforts to apply the antidotes to loneliness will emerge naturally and be more effective.

This letting go of well-intended efforts does not imply that an effortless pathway then lies ahead. Rather, we are simply breaking out of a reliance on brute force, an approach in which most of our energy is lost fighting the opposing forces within ourselves. Our attempt to break out of loneliness still calls for a commitment strengthened by patience and persistence. Then, whether we know it or not, the struggle within the self is over.

It's Okay to Feel Lonely

Fighting *against* our loneliness is the kind of "trying" that always backfires and creates more frustration. A more nourishing attitude, that it's okay to feel lonely, is a nonjudgmental recognition that loneliness is a part of our experience of the present. In this sense, breaking out of loneliness begins when we face our loneliness and allow ourselves to experience it fully. As we have already said, the resolution of loneliness cannot be achieved by trying to push it out of our lives; it is achieved by confronting ourselves with the reality of its existence and then breaking out of it by discovering new, more nourishing attitudes and behavior.

The attitude that it's okay to feel lonely does not imply a passive or helpless wallowing in loneliness. Rather, it is a willingness to accept without necessarily liking the reality of our loneliness and surrendering to it fully by giving up our attempts at games of denial and avoidance. The irony of this process, which is difficult for most of us to accept, is that by not trying to push away our feelings of loneliness, a resolution will emerge more readily. By giving up our programming, allowing ourselves to be lonely and accepting it nonjudgmentally, we confront ourselves fully with the reality of our experience—that we *are* lonely—and set the stage for the emergence of resolutions from within the self. When we do not deliberately expend effort and, instead, simply *allow* ourselves to be where we are, we break out of the well-intended but toxic patterns of self-manipulation.

Giving up our deliberate trying in order to see what happens when we surrender to ourselves and allow our own higher wisdom to emerge is an extremely threatening action. However, once we learn this form of self-trust and allow the self to unfold naturally without forced effort, truly creative resolutions and new ways of relating inwardly and outwardly begin to manifest themselves. These are our own unique creative processes in action. These are natural potentials for solving our dilemma, unfolding from within.

Do Something Scary

Living in chronic loneliness means living within a rigid set of attitudes and behavior patterns which dominate our personal lives and almost everything we do. Knowingly or not, we live a narrow, static existence which avoids natural growth and change. The more superficial aspects of our life do, of course, change through the years. We may move to new localities, develop new friends, or find new interests and activities. We may change occupations, wives or husbands, or various aspects of our life-style. These superficial changes are neither growth-producing nor effective antidotes to loneliness. In fact, we often wonder why such changes haven't affected our loneliness somehow. As long as our attitudes and behavior remain the same, as long as we continue to see ourselves and the world in the same old way, such occurrences and decisions remain inconsequential in resolving our loneliness.

> CHANGING SPOUSES, LOVERS, JOBS,
> FRIENDS, OR GEOGRAPHIC LOCATION IS
> IRRELEVANT IN OUR QUEST TO BREAK
> OUT OF LONELINESS.

To risk opening ourselves means venturing beyond established, often habitual attitudes and behavior patterns and facing what seems threatening if it *also* seems to offer new possibilities for discovery.

> WHEN WE EXPAND OUR INNER
> DIMENSIONS SOME PSYCHOLOGICAL
> PAIN IS INEVITABLE.

When we imagine we are taking risks, and yet do not feel any stress, anxiety, or threat, we can be fairly sure that no growth will occur. However, the converse, that whenever we experience pain we are growing, is not true. Most pain, like most tension, anxiety, and fear, is a waste of human resources and a manifestation of the suffering which comes from getting stuck with the endless frustration of behavior patterns. When we pay attention, we can differentiate pain that is an unavoidable part of growth and pain that is useless suffering from old, toxic patterns.

We have said that loneliness distorts our perception of reality. While we may be determined to do something about our loneliness, our "risk-taking" may turn out to be nothing more than a new version of the old attitudes and behavior which perpetuate our loneliness. We may sincerely believe we are reaching out for new growth when, in fact, we are continuing to bring our established patterns of self-induced loneliness into each new activity, relationship, and experience. When our loneliness persists in spite of these efforts, we become more confused. When through lack of greater awareness we continue to distort reality, we fail to realize that, psychologically speaking, we are still beating the same dead horse. Our frustration and despair continue to grow and we gradually lapse into deeper loneliness.

The antidote process of opening up to new possibilities means breaking out of the rigid attitudes and behavior that distort our perceptions of the new so that the possibility exists for something new to emerge.

> BREAKING OUT OF OLD ATTITUDES AND
> BEHAVIOR PATTERNS *IS* FRIGHTENING
> EVEN WHEN WE CLEARLY PERCEIVE
> THAT THEY HAVEN'T WORKED.

We recognize that the facades and defenses we have built are the real obstacles preventing us from obtaining the emotional nourishment we need to grow and resolve our loneliness.

> CHRONIC LONELINESS ALWAYS MEANS
> THAT OUR PERSONAL GROWTH PROCESS
> IS STAGNANT.

Pathways from Loneliness

None of us finds full satisfaction of every need, nor is this necessary to resolve our loneliness. For example, for some of us, developing a loving attitude toward ourselves can resolve loneliness without any further effort. Or, when we become involved in a mutually nourishing, intimate relationship, we may find our loneliness has lessened significantly. For some of us, discovering our love of humankind and dedicating ourselves to work for others may resolve our loneliness. Most of us are aware that these and other pathways can lead to the resolution of loneliness. At times, we may be aware that we are experiencing the nourishment that comes with our involvement in one or more of these areas and that our loneliness seems to have melted away entirely.

> WE GET STUCK WHEN WE FAIL TO SEE
> THAT DISCOVERING HOW TO NOURISH
> OURSELVES, HOW TO DEVELOP A
> GROWING MEANINGFULNESS AND
> EXCITEMENT IN OUR LIVES, IS NEVER
> A FIXED ACCOMPLISHMENT.

Often, for example, we believe the "and-they-lived-happily-ever-after" myth, and we decide that we have reached our goal or found the relationship we want and that our loneliness is finally over. Indeed, the emotional deprivation of loneliness often has vanished, but we fail to see that *any* resolution of loneliness is a process and that unless we continue to pay attention to our needs, emotional deprivation of various kinds will recur that can once again lead us into chronic loneliness. Without awareness of this process, we tend to seek more nourishment than is available from whatever resolution we have discovered. For example, when we find some degree of resolution to our loneliness through marriage but it eventually ceases to provide the gratification it once did, we may begin to focus more intensely on the relationship. We may become increasingly demanding or complaining about the failure of our spouse to meet our needs. This is a manifestation of our avoidance of exploring more of our own potentials in our quest for continuing growth. At the same time we do what we can to enhance the intimacy of our marriage.

Some of us have difficulty in accepting the fact that a relationship can be satisfying for a while but must be nourished by our own inner growth if it is to continue to be gratifying.

There are basic needs in each of us that can only be gratified by the limitless resources of our inner self.

When we feel sufficiently satisfied and secure in one area of life, a surplus of energy gradually builds up, along with a new pressure to move on. This energy *naturally* motivates us toward higher, more creative levels that tap new potentials. When we adopt this more comprehensive view, we begin to see that our growth process involves moving on from needs and goals that we may have struggled with most of our lives. When, for example, our needs for interpersonal intimacy are satisfied, other interests, activities, or goals become more dominant, and our attention and motivation naturally shift.

We are multidimensional. Each dimension has its unique need pattern. Each offers numerous antidotes to loneliness. The more dimensions of reality we incorporate into our lives (e.g., personal growth, intimate relationships, spirituality, etc.) the more meaningful our lives and, consequently, the less lonely we will be.

> THE PROCESS OF RESOLVING OUR
> LONELINESS ADVANCES WHENEVER WE
> DISCOVER NEW AND DIFFERENT
> DIMENSIONS OF HUMAN REALITY THAT
> ENHANCE THE QUALITY OF OUR LIVES.

In this way, we discover just how infinite the experience of being alive can be! This kind of fulfillment brings not only satisfaction but excitement and new energy as well. This newly released energy snowballs into new sources of nourishment and growth. Discovery becomes increasingly nourishing, meaningful, and effortless. In this ultimate antidote process loneliness simply falls by the wayside!

Psychological Rebirth and the Need to Understand

Breaking out of chronic loneliness is often experienced as a psychological rebirth. Breaking out from what has often been a lifetime of destructive attachments, anxieties, and fears, which, knowingly or not, we have carefully protected and nurtured, is not a complicated process. In fact:

VIEWING THE PROCESS OF BREAKING
OUT OF LONELINESS AS A COMPLEX
ORDEAL IS IN ITSELF A WAY OF
HOLDING ON TO OUR LONELINESS.

When we feel chronically lonely, we may analyze our loneliness in great detail, yet never feel that our analysis is complete. We may then decide that we need to try harder or that more or different psychotherapy will provide a more comprehensive explanation of "why" we are lonely and what caused it.

Actually, *trying* to understand is futile because we may never finish understanding a lifetime of past events. Today is tomorrow's past; our well-meant efforts at "understanding" may become interminable.

A RESOLUTION TO LONELINESS IS MORE
SIMPLY ACHIEVED BY BREAKING OUT
OF THE MYTH THAT OUR FEARS,
ANXIETIES, FEELINGS OF INADEQUACY,
AND SO FORTH MUST BE UNDERSTOOD
AND "CURED" BEFORE WE CAN
PROCEED.

The essence of growth is breaking out of the past, of the obsolete, of what is no longer nourishing (if it ever was) and moving on to a harmonious blending of ourselves with the reality of each new day. This kind of psychological rebirth has no prerequisites. It can occur innumerable times throughout one's life. In fact, many people do feel that they have changed to such an extent, often in a relatively short period of time, that they feel as if they were a different person. They know they will never be the same, and invariably they are glad of it.

Breaking out of loneliness by rebirth centers on sustaining our awareness of *how* we interrupt ourselves, lose contact with reality *in the moment,* and miss the excitement and vitality of the present by clinging to memories of past traumas or agonizing fantasies of future catastrophes. Or we can become aware of how our analysis literally paralyzes us both physically and psychologically, so that our behavior becomes increasingly artificial.

> TRYING TO UNDERSTAND CAN KILL OUR
> SPONTANEITY AND CAN LITERALLY
> TAKE AWAY THE JOY OF BEING ALIVE.

Most of us struggle all our lives with the same emotional problems. We keep searching for new insights, new understandings, and new solutions. Often enough we find ways that are helpful and that diminish our pain. There is, however, something circular about this process when we find ourselves endlessly trying to resolve it, yet somehow never getting finished. In this way we either wear out the problem or we wear out ourselves.

> OUR PROBLEMS WILL PERSIST AS LONG
> AS WE CONTINUE TO SEEK SOLUTIONS
> WITHIN THE SAME CONTEXT AS THAT
> IN WHICH WE CREATED THEM.

For example, the best way to create more pain and frustration is to focus on our dislikes. (Do you know what that S.O.B. did today?) By constantly complaining, more energy is fed into the situation, making it increasingly destructive, while we fail to move closer to a resolution. A more nourishing attitude is to accept our dislike. That is, cope with the situation as best we can, and then turn our attention elsewhere. We stop pouring energy into a stalemate when we shift our attention. We are also shifting our attitude about the problem, and in that way we can more easily break out of it.

With this shift in attitude comes a freeing of the energy that has been committed to such frustrating struggles. Instead, we allow ourselves to have our conflicts without insisting that they must be resolved, or even understood, and we move on to new levels of awareness and the discovery of new aspects of ourselves.

> INSTEAD OF BEATING OUR LONELINESS
> TO DEATH WITH ANALYSIS AND AN
> ENDLESS PREOCCUPATION WITH IT, WE

CAN SIMPLY BREAK OUT OF IT AND
MOVE ON TO SOMETHING NEW.

MARLIS:

I have always loved music. I was still in grade school when I began to pick out melodies on the piano and compose words to go with them. I enjoyed this immensely. Even then, I knew I would go into music. But my anxiety was so intense that I kept it a secret. When one of the family came into the room, I stopped playing. Eventually they moved the piano into a room over the garage, which made me feel a lot more comfortable.

I studied at a conservatory and was scared to death when I had to perform. My four years there were agony. I did a great deal of composing but rarely finished anything. When I did, it was because I had to meet some course requirement. Finally, I gave up trying to play in public or earn a living as a professional musician. My fears are still there, but I decided I didn't have to wait for them to disappear before I could move on professionally. Now I am a successful composer *and* I refuse to play for anyone! My new attitude carries over into other aspects of my life. I had always felt a great deal of loneliness; now I just allow myself to be lonely! I feel I have moved away from focusing so much on my problems. They just don't seem as important anymore.

The turning point for me came after a brief, disastrous marriage. I went to a therapist for three years, which was helpful. My insight deepened, but my fears and loneliness remained. At times I felt like a hopeless neurotic; I felt that I would have to forget any musical aspirations. When I composed something and became excited about it, my anxieties about performing it would overwhelm me and I would leave it unfinished.

It was chance that changed all this. I was badly injured in a car accident and confined in a body-cast for over a year. Out of boredom and loneliness I began composing again. Still, I could never finish anything to my satisfaction. Each time I gave up, I felt swallowed by my anxieties and sorry for myself for being so neurotic. This time, however, because of the months of confinement, and the boredom and loneliness I felt so intensely, I found myself picking up old, unfinished compositions and working them over. By the time the cast was removed, I had completed over twenty compositions. Most of these were eventually published, and I am now a successful composer. And I just won't play except in strict privacy.

My anxieties and insecurities are still there, and they may be there for the rest of my life. I don't know and I really don't care! The difference is that I no longer see them as obstacles. Now I see that I allowed my fears and loneliness to be stumbling blocks. The more I accept them and don't try to do anything about them the sooner they run their course. I have known for a long time that I create my own obstacles. Now I have discovered how I can break out of them too!

Marlis learned to allow her "hang-ups" to be there without feeling she had to do anything about them *and* she gave up trying to understand them. She discovered for herself that she was able to move on in spite of her anxieties and express her creativity.

Marlis now relates to her world more openly and no longer allows her "neurosis" to depress her. She became more loving and giving and her relationships are now much more nourishing. Her second marriage is deeper, more intimate than any relationship she has ever known.

Resistance, fighting against anything that we experience within ourselves or our world, is a way of getting trapped in a toxic struggle. Whatever repels us is, in reality, some part of ourselves that we have not fully integrated and accepted. When we have integrated parts of ourselves, whether they please us or not, we no longer need to struggle against them.

For example, when we accept our loneliness and believe that it's all right to be lonely, even though it is painful, we allow it to be there without condemning it or getting angry at ourselves about it. We may, of course, decide to do something to relieve it. But we no longer treat our loneliness as an enemy. In contrast, when we do not accept our loneliness, we struggle against it, protesting, getting angry, or criticizing ourselves. We stay stuck in the problem and actually intensify it by feeding new energy into it.

When we feel that there is nothing effective that we can do, one antidote is to move on to something else until something new emerges to be explored. This is the essence of what it means to function as best we can in the present.

Initially this may feel like blind groping, and it may be the best we can do at the moment to break out of a toxic pattern and the emotional stagnation it invariably creates. In the continuous unfolding of the present, any breaking out of these obsolete attitudes and behavior patterns creates a kind of psychic space, a fertile void. It is in this state of openness that the possibility exists for the emergence of new, more nourishing actions which can prove to be the antidotes to loneliness of lifelong duration.

17

~~~~~~

Saying Good-Bye to the Past

For each of us, especially when we are lonely, the past is a psychological trap in which we can keep ourselves imprisoned for a lifetime. When we choose to, we can always find needless past grievances to ruminate about. We can, for example, cling to our anger and resentment against others for the abuses, real or imaginary, which we feel they have perpetrated against us. We can also poison ourselves endlessly with feelings of guilt and shame about whatever we judge to be our past failures or misdeeds. The deadliness of clinging to the past is magnified when we realize its cumulative aspect. Today is tomorrow's past. Ultimately, it is just as deadly to ruminate about yesterday's regrets as it is to cling to our childhood resentments.

THERE IS NO NOURISHMENT IN THE PAST.

When we are lonely we may cling to the past with obsessive intensity. Sometimes even the suggestion of forgiving others for the pain they caused us is met with such a hostile response that it would seem we were being asked to surrender something precious. (I'll never forgive my parents for not giving me more love!) Breaking out of our blaming games by forgiving others puts the responsibility for our present loneliness where it belongs—on ourselves.

We have already assimilated anything of value from the past. Further clinging to the past by thinking about it, being angry about it, and so forth minimizes the possibility of new awareness. When we dwell on the past, we limit our availability to enjoy the nourishment of the ongoing present.

Whatever trauma each of us has experienced in the past is, in the present, nothing more than a collection of obsolete experiences and, believe it or not, distorted memories. They are now irrelevant and only further distort our perception of the present. When we project our past experiences on present relationships we prejudice (pre-judge) our perception of the present. When we project our past experiences onto each new relationship we thereby contaminate it with obsolete attitudes and reactions. By generalizing in this way, we make the present a repetition of the past. To the extent that we do this, we are not open to anything new. For example, although we realize intellectually that we may have felt used in the past, those we are involved with in the present did not cause our trauma; emotionally, however, we may be reacting exactly as if this were the case!

CLINGING TO THE PAST BLOCKS US FROM BEING FULLY AVAILABLE FOR POTENTIALLY NOURISHING RELATIONSHIPS AND MAKES THE LIKELIHOOD OF OUR INITIATING NEW RELATIONSHIPS EVEN MORE REMOTE.

Holding on to the past often means that we just don't believe that others will ever respond to us as we would like them to. Our fear from the past dominates us and we continue to believe that, should we break out of (forgive and forget) the pain of past traumas, we are simply asking for more of the same.

Any new experience involves taking risks to some degree. The possibility of rejection or disappointment always exists and can never be eliminated. Trying to assure ourselves that we won't be rejected is indulging a fantasy that can keep us stuck indefinitely. In resolving our loneliness it is essential to break out and rise above past traumas in order to be available for emotional nourishment now.

Working through past traumas is totally unnecessary. Breaking out of the past means letting go of the *emotional* impact of these experiences, rising above the guilt, anger, resentment, embarrassment, and other emotional pain associated with these experiences. Breaking out of the past is simple but not easy, because we must allow all these feelings and anxieties to exist and go ahead with our risk-taking ventures anyhow. Recognize that the past *is* the past, and it cannot be undone, and that its power to poison us in the present exists only to the extent that we continue to ruminate about it.

An Experiment in Breaking Out of the Past

Using the technique discussed previously, imagine someone seated opposite you in an empty chair: someone who has caused you emotional pain or whose rejection has left you feeling angry or lonely, for example, a former lover or a parent. Talk to that person as if he or she were actually present. Take the risk of expressing as much of your feelings as you can. Be especially aware of any impulse you would like to express and also want to avoid. Get in touch with as much anger and resentment as you can. Recall how unfair he or she was, how you were misunderstood, and so forth. Create your own script as you go along. Let yourself experiment. If some of your statements don't ring true, let them go and move on. Don't hold back! Even exaggerate! Be patient and take your time. If you get stuck, pause for a few minutes and start again. Stay with it until you feel sure that you have said all you have to say.

Now change seats and be the other person. Have him or her tell you about his or her inner pain and rejections. Play the part of that person telling you of feelings of being unloved or rejected by parents or others.

Now comes what is usually the most difficult and most

crucial part. *Forgive the person for everything!* Talk to him or her with understanding and love.

Tell the person you love him or her, that whatever their intent or purpose, you are going to give up judging them. While this final phase is the most difficult, the results can be extremely gratifying.

> FORGIVING OTHER PEOPLE IS NOT FOR
> *THEIR* SAKE; IT IS FOR OURSELVES.
> FORGIVING IS A PROCESS OF BREAKING
> OUT OF THE PAST.

This experiment is done in solitude, whether the person you are placing on the empty seat is available or not. Were the other person actually present, such dialogues would meet with the same frustrations and lack of communication and understanding that contributed to the difficulties or deterioration of the relationship in the first place. The other person often wouldn't even know what you are talking about, let alone agree with you, since he or she invariably perceived the relationship or trauma quite differently.

This technique usually calls for many repetitions, even when done with a professional therapist. Be patient and engage in the dialogue as often as you are willing to, whenever you feel like it. Arrange for the necessary privacy and freedom from interruption. It is of the utmost importance to keep in mind that in forgiving and being loving you are freeing *yourself* and your own trapped energy. As this becomes effective by repeated use, you will find yourself less intensely involved with past trauma and rejections. As the energy that has been locked into these past experiences again becomes available, its release may be experienced as a feeling of relief and peace, or excitement and exhilaration. Other emotional reactions range from tears of joy to tears of sadness. Crying, in particular, is a common reaction, since tears, like forgiving, are a melting process. The issue is allowing yourself to accept what *is*, that the past *is* past. Don't analyze or judge yourself; rather allow whatever emotions emerge from within to flow out fully and completely.

You will finish with your tears, your joy, or whatever else emerges when the wisdom of your body tells you; and it will. Like all growth processes this exercise calls for a measure of self-trust and willingness to be open.

It helps if we remember that it is our carryovers from the past that distort our experiencing of the present. Our expectations based on the past can dominate us to such an extent that we don't give others a chance. It is we who are stuck with our past and, knowingly or not, we project that past onto each new relationship.

The distortion of the present by clinging to the past becomes more powerful when disagreements or resentments occur. Even minor episodes may trigger the feeling that "here it is again!" Any friction, however slight, is seen as step one in the same old pattern, which is about to be repeated. This then becomes a self-fulfilling prophecy as our paranoia takes over and we watch for every slight sign of further rejection.

Boredom and Frenzy

Loneliness is frequently accompanied by confusion about what to do with ourselves. Similarly, loneliness and boredom often occur together. Our main preoccupation may be using up the present while we wait and hope for something better in the future. Meanwhile, we deliberately kill time in order to avoid feeling our boredom and loneliness. Killing time to escape boredom may ultimately lead to the opposite pattern: a state of frenzy.

Those who feel trapped in the boredom of their loneliness often see life as an hourglass, in which the sands of time are running out. This leads to greater anxiety and desperation since lonely people often feel that they have a lot of catching up to do. Their frenzy to make up for what they feel they missed is simply another way of holding on to the past. None of us can ever "catch up." The only antidote is to begin living *right now*. We cannot pack more nourishment or excitement in our lives without destroying the nourishing quality of what *is*. To try to do this is to create the frenzied behavior that is commonly observed in lonely people. When we refuse to accept the futility of such efforts we are apt to continue to feel that we should work even harder, thereby increasing the frenzy of our efforts.

THE MORE WE PUSH TO CROWD IN AS MANY EXPERIENCES AS WE CAN, THE LESS WE ACTUALLY EXPERIENCE.

When we talk about living now we mean allowing ourselves to experience what is happening *right at the moment*. We don't need to try to grab these experiences; we need only open ourselves by paying attention to them. That's all!

WHEN WE DEVOTE OUR ATTENTION FULLY TO BEING IN THE PRESENT, FEELINGS OF LONELINESS OR BOREDOM ARE IMPOSSIBLE.

An Exercise in Awareness

Set yourself comfortably in a room by yourself with the door closed. Focus your attention on your inner self by closing your eyes and feeling yourself breathing. Follow your inhalations and exhalations for a minute or two. Now begin to talk to yourself silently as if your voice emanated from your chest, the area around your heart. Say to yourself silently, over and over: "I love myself unconditionally." Allow yourself to feel this statement in your body rather than in your head and thoughts. Be aware of any difficulties you may find in saying it to yourself *and feeling* this self-love. Be especially aware of any feelings that may emerge in your chest area.

Often a feeling of joy and excitement emerges through the repetition of this simple statement. It clears the mind of the intellectual rumination that suffocates our feelings of being fully alive. This exercise is a simple form of meditation. It is a way of focusing our awareness on our inner self in a loving way. This can be done anytime.

THERE ARE NO PREREQUISITES TO
BREAKING OUT OF LONELINESS. WE DO
THIS AT ANY MOMENT WHEN WE ARE
BEING LOVING TO OURSELVES NOW, AS
WE ARE.

18

How to Be Alone, Not Lonely

All of us are alone in the sense that our physical body is separate from that of every other being. We are born alone and we die alone. No one can be fully with us in experiences involving separate physical selves. This fact is a basic source of the fear and anxiety that come with chronic loneliness and that cause us to equate loneliness with being alone. For most of us, aloneness, like loneliness, is to be avoided as much as possible. We live under the illusion that being alone has no value; that it cannot provide any psychological nourishment and is, in essence, synonymous with the emotional deprivation we experience in loneliness. This distorted view dominates our attitude toward solitude. We blind ourselves to the realization that solitude can be diametrically opposed to loneliness. Nourishing aloneness is what we usually refer to as solitude.

We have said that loneliness is a message from within the psyche calling for more awareness and responsiveness to vital needs. It is a manifestation of the law of psychological self-preservation. Our bodies react to loneliness in the same way they react to other deprivations. When we feel hunger or thirst and do not respond effectively, these deprivations become increasingly urgent. Similarly, the pain of chronic loneliness is a message of increasing urgency to respond to the lack of meaning and fulfillment in our lives.

How we obtain the nourishment we need from the world, or fail to, is a reflection of a more fundamental attitude of how we relate to ourselves and satisfy our needs through our own inner resources. When we have felt deeply lonely we have tended to respond to our loneliness largely or entirely by seeking resolution outside of ourselves.

Because of fear, anxiety, and lack of self-trust, we raise psychic barriers between various aspects of our inner self. This is a way of trying to disown our loneliness. We then look outside ourselves for the resolution of our loneliness while feeling the same distrust of others that we feel toward ourselves.

Only when we take the responsibility to learn how to be effective self-nourishers can we discover the abundance of our inner potentials for discovering deeper and deeper meaning to life. Our growing consciousness of new dimensions of reality can fill us with optimism and excitement.

THE EXPERIENCE OF BEING ALONE CAN
BECOME AN OPPORTUNITY FOR INNER
EXPLORATION.

It is ironic that when we feel chronically lonely and desperately want to believe that we have these untapped potentials within ourselves, we lack the necessary self-trust and willingness to experiment that could lead to discovering enormous possibilities for breaking out of our loneliness.

Warren was one of four children who grew up on a farm near a large city. From early childhood he was filled with excitement and interest about the world around him. He helped with the farm chores and particularly enjoyed working with his father. Warren often compared his childhood to living in a big toy store. When he was punished for some misbehavior, his parents sent him to his room. He was not about to reveal that this "punishment" was simply an opportunity to enjoy his solitude. He had always enjoyed spending long hours in his room reading, fantasizing, or working on various projects.

The dread we often have about being alone is in marked contrast to the discovery that the joys of solitude can be the most nourishing kind of experience. The highs that can be found in solitude are diametrically opposed to the extreme despair of intense loneliness. Most of us are taught that being with other people is better than spending our time alone. However, in Warren's case, for example, the *natural* joy of solitude begins with the awareness that, when we feel lonely, we are often afraid of being alone. Alone, we try to distract ourselves since aloneness means we are once again on the brink of loneliness. When we let go of this preconceived attitude, we can begin to open ourselves to those kinds of nourishment which can *only* be experienced when we are alone. And we can only believe this *after* we have found some of our latent abilities to turn inward joyfully. Without this discovery of the nourishment of solitude, we are likely to continue equating aloneness with loneliness. Then, no matter how meaningful such experiences might actually be, they are overshadowed by the fear that when we are alone, our loneliness is always in the background and may re-emerge at any time. We are apt to continue to avoid those occasions when we might be alone. And, of course, the last thing we would do is deliberately arrange time to be with ourselves.

THE FEAR OF BEING ALONE IS
LEARNED. IT IS AN UNNATURAL
ATTITUDE.

When we are willing to experiment with being alone, when we are willing to risk breaking out of our expectations that aloneness is too frightening to tolerate, we are ready to discover the nourishment that comes with changing loneliness into solitude.

Solitude, once we learn to appreciate it, facilitates our ability to come into deeper contact with ourselves and to discover, mobilize, and integrate our inner resources into fuller awareness. Our willingness to experience solitude and discover its vast potential for self-nourishment helps us break out of loneliness. Focusing inward is not only the most direct way of discovering more about ourselves but, in addition, is the most effective approach in learning how to relate to others in a mutually nourishing manner.

> OUR FEELING OF INNER CONTACT AND
> INTIMACY IS BASIC TO OUR ABILITY TO
> RELATE INTIMATELY TO OTHERS.

Solitude is necessary to discover and nourish those higher levels of consciousness which have a quality beyond and different from our psychological needs and interpersonal relationships.

> WITH GROWING AWARENESS OF THE
> LIMITLESS BOUNDARIES OF OUR OWN
> CONSCIOUSNESS THE INNER SELF
> BECOMES A CONTINUALLY AVAILABLE
> SOURCE OF ENDLESS NOURISHMENT.

All of us know our inner self to some extent. We talk to ourselves, love ourselves, depress ourselves. The more chronic our loneliness, the more it reflects our having ignored or rejected the ways of nourishing ourselves that remain beyond our present degree of consciousness. When we lack self-love and self-appreciation, it is difficult to believe this untapped inner richness even exists. Instead, our fantasy is apt to be one of fear that inner exploration will only intensify our feeling of inadequacy and lessen our self-esteem. Or even more threatening are fantasies that we will come upon horrible qualities that will confirm our long-standing feelings that we are "bad" or even evil. Unpleasant or frightening dreams are often misunderstood as a verification of these fears.

Solitude and loneliness are opposite experiences reflecting how we relate to ourselves when we are alone. The more loving, accepting, and trusting of ourselves we are, the more we move toward that end of the continuum characterized by the joy and meaningfulness of solitude. Solitude offers the opportunity for a total, unconditionally loving contact with ourselves and, subsequently, with the world. It readies us for fuller awareness and the discovery of a sense of belonging to something greater than ourselves and is, therefore, a powerful antidote to loneliness.

In contrast, the more we avoid ourselves, the more our paranoia, fear, and distrust dictate our existence, the more we move toward the despair and panic which we experience when we feel that being alone is synonymous with loneliness.

> THE CHRONICALLY LONELY RARELY
> ENJOY SOLITUDE, SINCE IT IS
> AUTOMATICALLY EQUATED WITH
> LONELINESS.

Solitude as an antidote to loneliness involves a shift in attitude, until being alone becomes less frightening. This is another kind of risk-taking experiment in which the nourishment of solitude can begin to emerge into the foreground as our attitude about being alone evolves.

> BREAKING OUT OF LONELINESS MEANS
> SHIFTING OUR ENERGY BY RISK-TAKING,
> IN WHICH WE SURRENDER INTO
> SOLITUDE AND QUIETLY DO NOTHING.

Solitude is nourishing aloneness. It is a source of energy transformation leading to a more loving communion with one's self. It is an opening of the self toward the self and consequently toward others as well and reflects the basic truth that:

> ALL LOVE BEGINS WITH SELF-LOVE.
> WHEN WE HAVE LEARNED TO
> EXPERIENCE SOLITUDE JOYFULLY WE
> ARE MANIFESTING THIS LOVE OF OUR
> SELF.

Solitude can be viewed as a form of meditation. It is a way of turning off the incessant activities of the mind. The constant flow of external stimuli is then minimal, while the center of awareness is quietly turned inward. In solitude, as in meditation, the flow of activity of the mind is greatly diminished. The quietness which comes from temporarily ceasing to respond to the external world is paralleled by a quietness within, as the mind slows its constant activity. In this silent state of active passivity, we simply allow whatever emerges to come into awareness without any effort. Solitude is a breaking out of "premeditated" behavior. The most difficult work is to avoid interrupting this process by our well-intended efforts and to stand out of the way. This is the necessary attitude in order to allow our inner self to emerge, as it will, in its own time.

Barbara had finally dissolved her agonizing marriage. For three years she had felt a growing anger and frustration as she attempted to communicate her discontent to a husband who didn't want to hear. The four months since she left him had been a frenzy of activity: finding an apartment, furnishing it, and taking care of all the things necessary to resuming a single life. The sheer physical demands, added to her usual responsibilities, had been exhausting. She decided to disconnect her phone and spend the weekend by herself.

Saturday she awoke with a smile on her face and a feeling of exhilaration which was almost unbelievable! She realized how much she needed to be alone and how rarely she gave herself this simple gift. This weekend was to be a feast of solitude. She would avoid contact with others and remain silent for two days. There was to be no busywork or chores, not even any of the usual activities she enjoyed but which might distract her from centering on her inner self. She planned to meditate and take long walks, which she knew deepened her contact with herself and helped unclutter her mind. For Barbara, being alone was an expression of her self-love. In the past she had experienced an inner balance, a sense of being centered and in touch with her deeper self. The tensions and anxieties of everyday living seemed to melt away. She knew how to enjoy the nourishment of solitude. When she returned to work on Monday she felt radiant and alive. People commented that she must have had quite a weekend. She preferred to keep the experience to herself, feeling that she could not convey its quality and that sharing might take away some of the precious energy and sense of well-being which continued to nourish her through the week. For Barbara, solitude was part of her life-style, an important form of self-nourishment, and an effective antidote not only for her occasional loneliness but for the pain of other emotional stress and tensions as well.

It is paradoxical that, because loneliness makes us so fearful of being alone, we ignore (remain ignorant of) the wealth of inner resources that could open us to greater awareness of our self and expanded meaningfulness in being alive.

The inner growth that comes with discovering the value of solitude is a form of self-therapy. When we have felt chronically lonely, this more open, trusting attitude and the increased self-awareness that follows set the stage for new insight into how we actually create the pain and anguish of our loneliness. It becomes clearer to us *what* we do to cause our loneliness and *how* we do it.

Solitude offers an opportunity for *going through* experiences of loneliness. In this approach, solitude is an active process, in which we do not try to do anything except allow ourselves to experience fully our loneliness simply by confronting it. We maintain contact with our feelings of loneliness and witness what unfolds from within. The acceptance of what we know from experience does exist, in this case our loneliness, is the optimal attitude for new insights and understanding to emerge, and with the insights, for more effective resolutions to follow.

An Experiment in Solitude

This procedure may be particularly useful when we are feeling lonely. Sit quietly alone in a room, eliminating as much noise and external stimulation as possible. Close your eyes and get your body in a comfortable position. Move as little as possible. Begin to contemplate someone you love, whether present or past, whether he or she is alive or not. Focus your attention at the level of your heart.

Think in a warm, loving way about that person, as if you were going to say how much you love (not miss) and care about him or her. Think of the joyful, nourishing experiences that you've had together. If you feel emotional or want to cry, give in to your feelings and allow them full expression.

Now that you have allowed yourself this release, experiment with a different resolution. Continue to feel your lovingness toward this person. As your feelings begin to well up, usually around the diaphragm or stomach, imagine yourself pushing these feelings up into your heart area. Allow them to fill your heart with love and hold these feelings there. Keep your heart open.

This exercise moves your energy from loneliness, depression, or emptiness into a loving attitude. The energy is transmuted into feeling more open and giving and, in turn, less isolated. It is a way of releasing energy from chronic emotional patterns that long resulted in nothing but feelings of depression, futility, and loneliness. It is an exercise in which we can let go of our particular self-poisoning attitude (self-pity, anger, futility, etc.) and transform this energy into feeling and being more loving. Being loving is the ultimate pathway toward breaking out of loneliness.

Be aware, when the experiment is over, if you resume poisoning yourself by wallowing in loneliness and self-pity; or whether you can accept and appreciate the nourishment that you just enjoyed and continue to integrate it by giving your lovingness a greater role in your total consciousness.

LEARNING TO ENJOY SOLITUDE BY TEMPORARILY CUTTING OFF EXTERNAL STIMULATION OPENS THE DOOR TO THE ESSENCE OF OUR EXISTENCE. IN NO OTHER WAY CAN DEEPER MEANINGFULNESS IN OUR LIVES BE SO DIRECTLY APPROACHED.

Typically, chronically lonely people are fearful of arranging their time to allow for periods of solitude. Most of us tend to fear that our loneliness will emerge like a black cloud and overwhelm us. We may see the quest for solitude as a deliberate tempting of the fates to bring down the doom of loneliness upon us, as if deliberately arranging to be alone is too threatening even to experiment with. It is ironic that these fears actually enhance the likelihood of loneliness.

Solitude, discovering the richness of our inner self, can make loneliness impossible. As one person put it: "How can I possibly be lonely when the richness I have found within myself seems to expand endlessly and remains continuously exciting?"

19

❧❧❧❧❧❧

Moving On and Breaking Out

Most of our inner processes, as well as our interactions with the world, take place with relatively little awareness. Our behavior is often automatic and reflects old attitudes and habit patterns rather than deliberate, more fully conscious actions. Our ability to discover creative resolutions to our problems lessens as our awareness lessens.

Awareness also means *paying attention* to what we are doing as we respond to our thoughts, feelings, and impulses. We are in touch with how we experience our actions and responses to these inner processes. To focus our awareness we can at any moment ask:

> IS THIS REALLY WHAT I WANT TO DO
> AT THIS MOMENT WITH MY TIME AND
> ENERGY?

Such simple questions, directed to ourselves in a loving manner, without being judgmental, can enable us to shift our energy and begin paying more attention to our attitudes and behavior patterns. Our awareness begins to grow and with it a shift from toxic to nourishing behavior. When we are plagued with the pain of chronic loneliness we can ask ourselves whether what we are doing at any moment alleviates, enhances, or is without effect on our loneliness. Continuing to be aware of the nourishing and/or destructive manifestations of our attitudes and actions *in an ongoing fashion* then becomes an integral aspect of our behavior. This is the self-correcting process that develops when we live in the present. There exists, then, a continuity of awareness of how we are functioning. We can ascertain continuously whether what we are doing is nourishing or toxic.

We need different kinds of nourishment to feed the diverse needs of our total self. When we are emotionally well nourished, we are more resistant to stress and toxic influence. Loneliness is never a static aspect of our existence. The intensity of our loneliness fluctuates. It too is a part of the unfolding process of our self.

When we feel like helpless victims trapped in our loneliness, this is a manifestation of the long-standing self-poisoning processes which we have created. Unless we intervene with new awareness and active experimentation, an ever-increasing preoccupation with our loneliness is most likely. While it is the last thing we intend, an obsession with loneliness only breeds more loneliness. We continue to channel more and more energy into the problem in the same old ways. Without exploring new possibilities we can never discover the infinite potentials each of us has for breaking out of our loneliness and moving on. The alternate approach is to shift our attention and energy in new and different directions. In our quest for something new, we must first break out of our old obsessive attitudes about our loneliness, which we recognize by their monotonously repetitious quality.

BREAKING OUT OF LONELINESS IS A CONSEQUENCE OF CONTINUOUSLY TAKING THE RISK OF MOVING ON IN NEW DIRECTIONS.

Never Surrender

Since every aspect of life is process, the idea of giving up the quest for what we need is totally unrealistic. One way or another, whether we are aware of it or not, change occurs continuously. The central issue in breaking out of loneliness is choosing to take responsibility for how we live our lives. The possibilities for discovering antidotes to loneliness are always present when we center our awareness on our own inner processes. To give up this freedom of self-determination is to surrender ourselves to fate and the whims and hang-ups of other people.

> THE COMMITMENT NOT TO SURRENDER
> TO OUR FEARS, ANXIETIES, AND
> INSECURITIES OPENS US TO
> DISCOVERING ANTIDOTES THROUGH
> EXPERIMENTING WITH NEW ATTITUDES
> AND BEHAVIORS.

All pathways from loneliness lead toward joy and satisfaction and a feeling of belonging.

> LONELINESS FADES AWAY WHEN WE
> FEEL THAT WE BELONG.

A meaningful, creative resolution to loneliness is experienced as an evolution of our attitudes and behavior patterns. As the emotional deprivation of our loneliness begins to wane and we discover more of our latent potentials, we become more our own person. A new, more solid feeling of connectedness with others emerges and becomes an additional catalyst to growth. Our life grows more meaningful and more creative. We become increasingly nourishing to others. As these nourishing cycles flourish, the pain and anxiety of loneliness recede into the background.

> AWARENESS IS SYNONYMOUS WITH
> GROWTH. ONCE WE SEE THE GAMES
> THAT CREATED OUR LONELINESS, WE
> ARE AWARE OF THEM FOREVER.

Indeed, we can no longer escape into old patterns and avoid new awareness, even if we want to. The nourishing self continues to press relentlessly and confronts us over and over again with the phoniness and emptiness of our patterns of self-induced loneliness. Gradually, at our own pace and in our own time, these toxic patterns become more and more nauseating as we become more aware of their poisonous effect.

In the final analysis, the wisdom to know how to resolve our loneliness has always existed. We simply were never willing to face up to it! With a new attitude of self-acceptance, self-love, and self-trust that what we are seeking *is* available, our games of loneliness become obsolete and melt away.

Whatever the extent of past traumas and rejections or present insecurities and fears about reaching out for what we need in the here-and-now, the possibilities of breaking out of loneliness are always present. The innate nourishing qualities within each of us, the natural healthy openness and responsiveness each of us is born with, remain within us always, pushing for expression. Feelings of helplessness and hopelessness are only a manifestation of the obsolete protective devices which we have created and which only lead to isolation and alienation. Believing we must wait for these obstacles to disappear, or that we must undergo some metamorphosis to release ourselves from the prison we have created, is fantasy.

Experimenting, in spite of the presence of old fears and anxieties, takes courage. Once we are aware that we ourselves are causing our emotional pain and sustaining our loneliness, this awareness, together with our courage and will to survive and grow, can bring us to a point where we take risks and learn to move on. Our process of growth then resumes naturally and old fears and anxieties begin to diminish. They need never disappear. This is a false myth of perfectionism. At any moment we can do what we want to do in spite of them. We can face up to what we need. We can reach out to others who are as eager for contact as we are.

> AS WE BECOME LESS TOXIC AND MORE NOURISHING WITHIN OURSELVES WE WILL FIND THAT THE WORLD AROUND US ALSO BECOMES INCREASINGLY NOURISHING. THIS IS BREAKING OUT OF LONELINESS.

We can consolidate our whole perspective by keeping in mind the underlying framework within which each of us can strive in doing the best we can to resolve our loneliness.

BREAKING OUT OF LONELINESS BEGINS AND ENDS WITH OURSELVES.

When we are lonely, the initial issue is to confront ourselves with our own deprivation. As we develop our inner potentials, we learn how to reach out more effectively to the world to obtain what we need. We use our inner resources as the basis for any resolution of our loneliness. We discover that mobilizing our inner self is our most effective way of learning how to reach out to the environment and seek the kind of relationships with other people that we find nourishing and satisfying.

This process is never a smooth one. All of us go through periods of emotional feast and famine to one degree or another. Each time we begin to feel deprivation or frustration, the basic and most effective action is to return again to our inner self by centering our awareness within ourselves and re-examining our own attitudes and behavior patterns. We turn inward to regroup and rally our inner strength. This process in itself is very nourishing. Through it we discover our own power to resolve our loneliness, as we begin again to mobilize our energies and again take new risks.

The best we can do is to return continuously to the source of our basic mental, emotional, and spiritual power—our inner self. Whenever we feel trapped or lonely, our main attention remains inner-directed. This is the essence of taking full responsibility for ourselves. It is a statement of responsibility for everything we do. It is also a statement of self-trust and love and commitment to the truth: that each of us has all the answers inside, that we lack nothing that we need, that the resolution of our loneliness always awaits the discovery of these answers which lie dormant within our deeper selves. The time to break out of our loneliness is now.

Index

Gratitude, and rescuers, 66
Grievances, from past, 30–34
Growth
    and awareness, 220
    and self-acceptance, 19–20
Guilt, and punishment, 97–99

Helplessness, 113
    as distortion of reality, 92
    and suicide, 58
    see also Emotional cripple
        fantasy; Impotence
Humor, as antidote, 182–183
Hurt, psychic, 110–111

Image, idealized, 72–73, 179
    see also Self-image
Impatience, 35–37
    vs. patience, 189–190
Imperfection, and expectations,
    19
Impotence
    and paranoia, 109
    and suicide, 58
    see also Helplessness
Inadequacy, and odd-ball syn-
    drome, 88–90
Individualism (rugged), over-
    valuation of, 134–135
Initiating (toxic), of relation-
    ships, 63–65
Inner intimacy, 9–13
Inner self, exploration of, 77–
    78, 212, 214, 217
Insight (psychological), misuse
    of, 68–72
Insomnia, 76–77
Integration, 40, 173–174, 200
    see also centering
Intellectualizing, psychological,
    68–72
Interests, 106
Internal orientation, vs. external
    5–6, 187–188
Intimacy, 7
    inner, 9–13

limited, 174
vs. manipulation, 51
vs. ostrich syndrome, 80–81
and sexuality, 117–120, 123–
    124
single, 48–51
Introversion, and extroversion,
    99–100

Judgmental attitude, and projec-
    tion, 51

Known, vs. unknown, 40

Laughter, as antidote, 182–183
Learning
    avoidance of, 44–46
    and fragmentation, 154
Living
    and death, 142–146
    fear of, 58
Loneliness, 4
    acceptance of, 192
    denial of, 5
    hiding, 27, 29
    myths, 94–107
    patterns of, 61–63
    see also Antidotes
Lovability, 180
    need to prove, 11–12
    and "you first" game, 74
Love
    and caring, 140–141
    and self-love, 10, 213
    see also Giving; Nourishment
Lovingness, 179–180, 216

Mañana syndrome, 86–88
Manipulation
    vs. authentic relating, 51–52
    complaining as, 91
    giving as, 52–56
    and professional psychologiz-
        ing, 71–72
    and rescuers, 66

Manipulation (continued)
  and toxic attitude, 16–18
  see also Game-playing; Ostrich syndrome
Marriage, 130–133
  and commitment, 127–129
  expectations of, 125–126
Material success, goal of, 34
Meaningfulness, creating, 57
Meditation, 207
  and solitude, 213–214
Men
  loneliness of, 100, 103, 104
  sexuality of, 120
Middle years, 103
Motivation, 191
  and energy, 196
  and patience, 189, 190
  and risk-taking, 159–160
Mourning, and loss, 170
Myths, of loneliness, 94–107

Narcissism, 83–84
Negative attitude. *See* Toxic attitude
"New Year's resolutions," 86–87
Nourishing attitude, vs. toxic attitude, 14–16, 18–21, 48–51, 92, 126–127
Nourishment, 195
  of emotional pain, 174–175
  of solitude, 26–27, 209–217
  see also Giving; Love; Self-love

Objects, people as, 52
Odd-ball syndrome, 88–90
Older people, 103–105
Openness, 165–166
Orientation: internal vs. external, 5–6
Ostrich syndrome, 79–83, 156–157
Others, 105
  and intimacy, 174

Packaging, of personality, 6, 52
Pain. *See* Emotional pain
Pandora's Box attitude, 9–10
Paranoia, 105, 165
  and fear of rejection, 108–111, 114–116
  and perception, 163–164
  and vulnerability, 111–112
Parental rejection, in childhood, 39
Parents
  and children's disappointment, 85
  and emotional cripple fantasy, 41
Passive relating, 67–68
Past experiences, 30–34, 202–204
  and forgiveness, 205
  and paranoid projection, 112–113
Patience, vs. impatience, 189–190
Perception
  and fragmentation, 154
  and paranoia, 115–116, 163–164
Perfectionism, and criticism, 86–88
Phobic attitude, toward rejection, 38–40
Physical attractiveness, 100–103
Play, of young children, 25
Poisonous attitude. *See* Toxic attitude
"Poisonous words," 19
Positive attitude. *See* Nourishing attitude
Privacy, and adolescence, 25
Problems, quick solutions for, 35–37
Procrastination, and perfectionism, 86–88
Professional psychologizing, 68–72